THE HOUSES OF CLEBURNE COUNTY

Memoir of a Southern Boyhood

WILLIAM CARROLL MOORE

The Houses of Cleburne County
by
William Carroll Moore

Published by: Nicasio Press
                 Sebastopol, California
                 www.nicasiopress.com

Cover Design: Mandy Masciarelli Design
                 mmdesignnapa.com

ISBN: 979-8-9897756-0-6
Printed in the U.S.A.

Dedication

To my sister, Helen Marie; my brother, Alder Lee; and to our late parents, Melba and Carroll Moore for the wonderful life they gave us. Also, to the people of Cleburne County whose stories , in their soft voices, are still in my ear.

Acknowledgements

My abundant thanks go to the members of my writers critique group: Sue Kesler, Gary Orton, Michael Wycombe, Sarita Lopez, Rose Winters, and Marty Malin, for their friendship and patient, valuable help. Thanks also to my beta readers, Lance and Susan Burris.

Much appreciation goes to the publication *Time and the River*, a history of Cleburne County by Evalena Berry, which was a helpful resource in anchoring my memories to places and dates.

CONTENTS

INTRODUCTION

In February, 1983, Cleburne County, Arkansas, celebrated its 100th year. The Centennial delegation presented a copy of the just published county history, *Time and the River*, and a newly-minted commemorative silver coin to Governor Bill Clinton at the 74th General Assembly of the State of Arkansas. Included in the Centennial observance was an address, *Brief Glimpses into Our Past*, by Dr. Bert Stark, Jr., Professor, University of Central Arkansas, Conway. The following is an excerpt from his address:

"Time passed, and in 1930 the greatest depression in the history of our country occurred. Drouth, no market for crops and livestock created an extreme shortage of money. These were extremely hard times. The Works Progress Administration was conceived.

"Again, time passed, and World War II was here. Many of you will recall that this was a period of great social upheaval in this county. Again, hundreds of our sons enlisted or were drafted into the military services —some of them did not return. Hundreds of others left our county and scattered to the four winds to work in war plants, some of them never to return to live here permanently.

"Then after the war a new social and economic scene was found. Small farms and row crops were no longer a viable agricultural venture. Many young people left the county to seek work elsewhere, and our citizens began to seek other means of livelihood."

As the son of an Arkansas farm family, I am able to give a first-hand account of how Cleburne County families and individuals met the challenge of the changing times outlined above by Dr. Stark. I lived through those very changes, from my time in a one-room schoolhouse, to participating in my family's struggle to survive, and at the age of ten, migrating with family to the Central Valley of California to start a new life.

This collection of stories represents a small window into the changes that shaped both Arkansas and the nation. I hope you enjoy reading them.

1924 - 1932

PART I . THE HOUSES BEFORE ME

THE HOUSES BEFORE ME

My family lived in eight houses in Cleburne County, Arkansas, where my parents were born, grew up, got married, and lived until I was ten years of age. Given the time and place—during the Depression of the 1930s—they moved from farm to farm, trying to get a purchase on life. The first five of these houses were before my unanticipated entrance into this world. These were the houses before me.

THE GRESHAM LITTLE HOUSE

My parents, Melba Adrid Gresham and William Carroll Moore, were secretly married the day after Christmas in 1924. Other than the justice of the peace who married them, only Mother's friend and witness, Carmen Gunn, knew of the wedding until the announcement at a family gathering some days later. My brother, sister, and I never understood why they held the wedding in secret, and our parents declined to comment. Though never stated, we finally assumed, or at least I did, that Dad would have had difficulty getting permission from Mother's father, John Anderson Gresham, Jr., as Dad, at that time, had neither money nor land, and Mother was not yet eighteen years of age. She had, quite correctly, made this risky choice to become the lifetime partner to this handsome, charming, and industrious man whom she already knew she simply could not live without (her words).

The secret marriage seemed ironic as Mother's father had been—or perhaps still was at that time—justice of the peace for the Pearson community where the Gresham family lived. In later years, Mother told me how as a young girl, on some of the many buggy trips with her father, he stopped the buggy at the side of the road, asked her to hold the reins, and disappeared into the nearby woods for some time. At first, she thought he had been disappearing to relieve himself, but later realized he had, as justice of the peace, been performing secret weddings in the shadows of the oak forest. We were never clear how our parents' marriage was received by her father, who had clearly been one-upped by another justice of the peace, one Claude Jones.

* * * * *

My parents started their life together in the small cottage we called the "Little House" on the Gresham family property near the town of Pearson. It was a two-story cottage built by my grandfather John Anderson Gresham, Jr. in 1906. The cottage had a certain beauty in its simplicity. The downstairs had a kitchen and dining room at the north end and a living room in the south. The two were separated by an entryway with the front and back doors and a stairway to the second floor, which had a bedroom on each side of the stairs. The cottage was a wood frame, board-and-batten structure with a cedar-shingle roof. It stood in a level area facing the road and meadow beyond and backed up to the edge of a woods.

Long before my parents moved in, it had been used as a temporary residence by my grandfather and his new wife, Sarah Helen Thompson Gresham, as a "weaner" house, as it has been for other family members just starting out on their own as my parents were. It has also served as temporary housing for farm workers. I don't know the circumstances of my parents' stay—whether Dad farmed the surrounding land or not—but after two years, they moved to a house on Kimbrough Lane where Dad leased land for his farming operation.

KIMBROUGH LANE

None in our immediate family, except our parents, ever saw the Kimbrough Lane house, or even knew where it was. Old man Kimbrough and his son owned two houses on the mountain property, and both they and their families lived in one house. Mother and Dad rented the other, which stood, we were told, in a windy area facing the road going from Heber Springs over to Pangburn. It had previously been used for storage of hay and wasn't well suited for habitation, as it was drafty and difficult to heat.

The house was barely livable but the farmland that came with it was productive, with enough acreage for Dad to hire help with harvests. My sister, Helen Marie, —or "Sis," as my brother and I call her—was born there in March of 1928, in a room whistling with cold. Our family never took us to visit the place, and I suspect they never wanted to see it again. They lived there for several years before their move to the Badders Place.

THE BADDERS PLACE

In 1930, our family moved in and shared a house with a widower, Tom Badders, and leased his land for farming. Badders was starting a poultry production operation on part of the property and didn't want to farm the land. He was convinced that the broiler chicken industry was the coming thing and would soon be a big business in the county, and maybe even in the whole state.

The house was arranged in a bungalow plan with one half having a living room, dining room, and kitchen in the one side; and two bedrooms and a screened utility porch in the other. It had a deep front porch facing north to the road and a large barn across the road. My sister was just beginning to walk when they moved there. Both operations—land crops and poultry farming—went well, but after three years, Badders decided to re-marry and needed the whole place for his larger family. Our family then moved to the Taylor Place.

THE TAYLOR PLACE

I know little about the Taylor Place, but from stories of their two years there, it seemed to be a very happy place for my parents. They endured two deep, cold winters there and spent many hours with their friends and neighbors living nearby. Dad installed sled runners under a wooden soap box with a rope-pull to transport little Helen Marie over the snow and ice to visit neighbors for taffy pulls and apple-bobbing parties.

During their stay at the Taylor Place, one of Dad's main jobs was head carpenter for the construction of a new house for Mother's dad, J. A. Gresham, Jr., on the Gresham Road property, where our family later lived, and where it still stands. Dad also learned the side job of barbering. Men came to their house every Saturday for haircuts in ever-increasing numbers. Mother complained that if Dad didn't leave home before noon on Saturdays, their house became a public place. Dad solved the problem by renting a chair in Lawson Roberts' barber shop in Pearson. This solved the domestic problem, and we're told Roberts enjoyed the extra traffic. During this time, we don't know if Dad kept farming the Badders land or the land that came with the Taylor Place. From here the family moved to the Coe farm, owned by Dad's family.

THE COE FARM

The Coe farm, which belonged to Dad's grandfather Robert Franklin Coe, and where Dad grew up from boyhood, covered a large, farmed acreage and had several houses on the property. Our family lived in what they called the "Simmons House," built by Dad and his granddad to house Dad's aunt Nancy and her husband, Walter Simmons. Mother described the house as having two 16-foot-square rooms under a gable, with a lean-to kitchen room on the back. While there, my sister, Helen Marie, attended the McAnear School where Mother,

her sister, and two of her brothers had attended years before. During their stay at the Simmons house, our family bought a parcel of land we call the "Jackson Place."

1932 - 1940

PART II.
THE JACKSON PLACE;
THE BETTIS PLACE

THE JACKSON PLACE

The Jackson Place was the most important of the houses our family occupied while living in Cleburne County. For my parents, it was important as the first home they had purchased, and it was important for me because I was born there. Our folks had moved from house to house, always hoping to someday have a farm of their own. There was difficulty finding a habitable house that also had enough farmland to produce viable crops. It was in the depth of the depression and times were tough, so they didn't know how or when they would find a suitable farm on a permanent basis with a good lease, or better still, one they could buy. That opportunity came in 1932 with the Jackson Place. They bought the forty-acre parcel and built a house and barn the same year. At the time of purchase, they still lived on the Coe farm, and continued living and farming there during the time Dad built the Jackson property and worked on both farms. I have no recollection of the Jackson house, but Mother filled me in over the years as to how the family fared during the early years.

I was born William Carroll Moore, Jr. in the Jackson Place, an unexpected child in a reluctant birth, during the Great Depression and at the height of the worst drought in our county's history. I was delivered by Dr. A. B. Wood on a second trip to our house. Mother was in labor so long that he delivered two other babies —one of them a complicated birth—during the wait. Mother said when they finally got to me, both she and Dr. Wood were so exhausted she hoped I would arrive undamaged. Although unplanned, I was received as a blessing and couldn't have been a more welcomed child.

* * * * *

Trees covered most of the Jackson property, mainly pines, with a thicket of cedar in one area. Once cleared, the land was suitable for farming—flat but well drained, and with productive soil. Dad began by clearing and grubbing six acres, enough for some crops, a meadow, garden patch, orchard, house, and barn.

In the cedar thicket, he made a brush fence to contain the livestock by cutting halfway through the cedars and bending them down, making a living fence of dense foliage. He cut enough of the pines to provide timber for construction of the house, and he hauled the logs by wagon to the mill where they were sawn "on the halves," leaving half of the timber with the mill to pay for the milling. He cut blocks from cedar logs and took them to the mill to be sawn into shingles, also on the halves. The house he built was a 16' by 28', two-room, board-and-batten structure with a shingled roof. He also built the doors and most of the furniture, including a dining table with benches, a library table for the living room, and the kitchen cabinets. For furnishings, they had to buy only the cast-iron bedsteads as well as a cast-iron and sheet-metal stove for both cooking and heating. The log barn was almost as big as the house and square. Dad sawed logs on the property to build it and made the cedar roof boards himself by splitting shingles from blocks of cedar. The building had a corncrib, a hayloft, two stalls for horses, and a lean-to shed added later to shelter the cattle.

Availability of water was a concern, as there was no well or spring on the property. My parents located a spring-fed branch nearby at the edge of their property but not within it. They used water from the branch, but for a secure water source, Dad planned to dig a well once crop production stabilized. With the help of a water witcher, he had selected the well site before building the house.

Dad was very good at growing things but was always interested in learning more and better methods for farming. It seemed natural that he became well-acquainted with the Farm Cooperative Extension agent for our county, one Harry Woodruff. He had known Woodruff for some time, and they met occasionally to discuss plant varieties, fruit tree husbandry, and the care and feeding of livestock. He had consulted Woodruff some years before when he helped my maternal grandfather Gresham plant his elaborate orchard on the Gresham Place and consulted him again for the Jackson Place orchard. With his guidance, Dad used root stock from the Gresham orchard and other places for several fruit varieties.

One of his experiments was grafting both Red Delicious and Yellow Delicious apple shoots to the same Johnny Apple root stock from the Gresham orchard. In addition to the apple plantings, he obtained other bare-root planting stock, with the help of Woodruff, for a total of eight fruit trees. In addition to apple, those included pear, peach, and red cherry.

Several grape vines were also included in the plantings, and he retained a patch of wild persimmons found on the property. As the plantings flourished, Dad claimed he could taste the fruit each time he looked at his young trees.

Establishing a home and farm in the depths of a depression was challenging enough, but droughts made things worse for the new farm. I'm told that the years 1934 through 1936 were drought years—1934 being the worst—so crops did not do well. At that time and place, there was no food welfare system for help, and people had to grow enough food to feed themselves. Dad's sorghum crop failed, and he had to trade work for canes from someone else for our molasses, the essential home-grown sweetener for baking and breakfast syrup. My widowed, paternal grandmother, Elizabeth Coe Moore, moved in to help with three-year-old Helen Marie and my infant self. She also planted and tended a vegetable garden, picking the vegetables as they grew to make into soup. The corn crop produced only nubbins, but the family made do by shelling the edges to feed the pigs, and taking the rest, a peck at a time, to the mill for cornmeal. Flour wasn't always available, so all bread was from cornmeal, meaning corn hoecakes for breakfast.

Dad was able to harvest some hay from the new meadow and store it in the hayloft for animal feed, but the supply wasn't sufficient. As the supply dwindled, our family feared losing livestock from starvation. Well into the winter, however, they noticed the cattle had begun to look fat and sleek. While out hunting, Dad discovered an abandoned sorghum mill on an adjacent property, and what had looked like a rubbish pile was actually a left-over pile of processed sorghum canes—a pummy pile. The cattle had strayed into the area and were eating the rich pummies, which was good feed for them, so no livestock was lost.

Among old family documents, I found a "Chattel Mortgage with Power of Sale" Dad executed with Arkansas National Bank in March 1935 and payable in mid-October of the same year. The loan must have been for the last crop he farmed on the Jackson Place. To borrow the $75 he needed to make his crop, he pledged essentially everything he owned as collateral:

One black horse mule, 12 years old, weight 800#
One black mare mule, 12 years old, weight 800#
Two jersey cows, 3 and 4 years old

John Deere wagon and one set double harness complete with collars, bridles, etc; Oliver cultivator; Avery breaking plow; Moline planter; also all single stocks and other farming implements now owned by me or that I may hereafter secure before the full payment of this mortgage.

I know he paid off the chattel mortgage because he had the same equipment some years later. The mortgage on the property itself was the big problem.

Our family lived in the Jackson house for three years before losing the whole farm to foreclosure. The loan was held by a member of a local family who put himself forth in the community as a "Good Christian."

He foreclosed on our family when they couldn't come up with $200 they were short to make a payment on time and couldn't get a loan from the bank. He wouldn't take a partial payment or give them an extension and benefitted from three years of our family's purchase payments, hard work, and best efforts improving the property. Our family had to leave before their orchard had borne its first fruit. Afterwards, they never spoke his name again, always referring to him not by name, but as "The Good Christian."

* * * * *

My schoolmates pointed out to me that my forefingers on both hands were scarred with what looked like burn marks, something I'd not noticed before. It was first told to me at an apple-bobbing party at the Bittle's house where we young folks, including nine-year-old kids like me, were playing parlor games, one of which was "Take a walk" or something like that. It was a random thing, like "spin the bottle" for a kiss. The "It" person, a young girl, was blindfolded and held out both hands, palms up. Two boys placed an index finger in each of her hands, and she was to grasp one finger. She selected mine, and we were assigned a walk together to the next farmhouse down the road and back. During the walk, she told me she could see under the blindfold and selected me, as she knew the scarred finger was mine.

The next day I examined my fingers in more detail and asked Mother how I got the scars. She told me that when I was little-bitty I had an accident when we lived at the Jackson Place.

"I'm glad you don't remember it," Mother said. "It was horrible."

She said it happened when I was playing in a ladder-back chair next to our iron-and-sheet-metal stove. With knees in the chair seat and hands grasping the top rail of the back, I was rocking to-and-fro. A forward rock too far tilted me into the stove, where my fingers were pressed to the hot metal and held there by my weight. My screams alerted Mother, who pulled me off the stove, leaving my smoldering skin on the hot metal, smelling of roasting pork. At the time, she was grief-stricken, having allowed such a thing to happen. It was also traumatic for my sister, Helen Marie. She added to Mother's story, relating that following the burn I was a happy little boy, with both hands bandaged like white boxing gloves, holding them in the air and walking around the house repeating three words: *Boochie, Boochie, Whooee! Boochie, Boochie, Whooee*! Now was Sis's chance to ask me what the words meant, as she had always wondered. I had no idea, of course, having just heard of them myself. I regretted I wasn't clever and quick enough to deliver an interesting and memorable translation.

I asked Mother why she hadn't told me about this event before.

"Some things are better unremembered," she said.

* * * * *

One evening at the Jackson Place, Dad had finished his chores and sat near where Mother was preparing dough to make biscuits for supper. As she was pouring buttermilk onto a layer of flour, folding them together and flattening the dough for cutting into biscuits, she lamented having no rolling pin for the task. Dad reached into the firewood box next to his chair, found a small log the right diameter and length, peeled off the bark with his knife, drove a large spike nail into each end and handed it to Mother. She used it for years before buying a regular rolling pin. I had never seen the handmade device until many years later when Dad was gone, and I was helping her move from their Santa Cruz, California, home to a condominium she had purchased. When I found it, she told me this story and explained; "It was such a loving thing he did for me, I can't bear to part with it. And," she said, "I'll be taking it with me today."

The Bettis Place

We are told the autobiographical memory in children starts at about three years of age. I may have been slow off the mark, as I can remember very little prior to the age of four when our family lived in the Bettis Place—the beginning of my recollection of time, place, and the world itself.

Our family leased one of the Bettis family farms, a forty-acre spread adjacent to the one the Bettis family themselves lived on. Our farm was located some three miles northeast of the town of Quitman, with a frontage on what is now State Road 25. The house hadn't been occupied for some time and was a bit run-down. It was a wood frame, board-and-batten structure with most of the paint weathered away, and the clay mortar eroded from the fieldstone chimney. It was still a good solid structure but clearly a mere shadow of its former self. From some distance back and squinting, one might have seen a faded vision of a yellow house with white window and door trim and white porch columns. The square shape of the columns was a tip-of-the-hat to a Neo-Greek style of architecture seen frequently in the South.

The farmhouse was built into the south slope of the hill. I assume its placement was to avoid the main force of storms on the hilltop, yet high enough up the hill to catch the cooling breezes of summer—a siting typical for many of the farmsteads in Cleburne County. The square-columned front porch extended across most of the façade. The living room and bedrooms were in the front part of the house, with a kitchen and back porch built in an L-shape off the back. The slope of the hill allowed space below the kitchen for a stone-walled lower story. We used this space for storing firewood and as a small workshop and tool storage for Dad. From the entry porch, there was a dogtrot opening—a covered, open passage—separating the living and sleeping areas of the front part of the house and connecting directly to the back porch, which gave access to the kitchen behind. The living room had a fieldstone fireplace at the east end. A solarium, which formerly may have been a screened porch, was attached to the north wall of the living room. I slept there and shared it with my paternal grandmother, Elizabeth, when she came to visit, and later, I shared it with my younger brother, Alder Lee.

The barn was further up the hill from the house and slightly over the ridge, on the west slope of the hill— the opposite slope from our water source. Downhill from the east side of the house, the access road from the highway ran parallel to a wooded creek branch fed by a robust spring on the property, which fed and added substantial flow to a smaller stream from the hills above. The spring itself, which was another reason for siting the house on this part of the property, was sheltered by a Victorian-style spring house, with a side door access. The downstream end of the spring house was filled with a wooden latticework from the gable down almost to the water, keeping animals away from the stored food and the fresh, cool water, which roiled continually from the ground. Slightly further downhill from the kitchen, on the west slope, a smokehouse and privy completed the farmstead.

Mother remarked from time to time how habitable the house was compared to the other houses they had lived in since their marriage. It had its drawbacks, but at least wind didn't streak through the walls and window casings as it had in Kimbrough Lane. As we settled in, I remember the house becoming more livable with continuing repairs by Dad, and handmade curtains and other amenities, such as a kitchen garden and flower beds, provided by Mother. It was the first place I remembered as home. My brother, Alder Lee, was born there in November 1938, delivered by Dr. Birdsong. When Dad brought me into the room and Mother introduced me to him, I'd never seen her look happier, and I felt proud to have a little brother.

A WINTER'S TALE

"I'm back from the store," Dad said as he walked into the kitchen. He had dropped off more of our farm products—butter, eggs, and cheese—for sale at the store, and cans of cream to be hauled to the Heber Springs creamery.

"I saw Randy Renfrow there; he said his brother Ed wanted to see me pretty soon, and could I come this week."

"Why wouldn't Ed come here?" Mother asked.

"He said Ed's wife, Effie, was sick, and Ed didn't want to leave her alone."

Mother and Dad pondered this request. Ed Renfrow owed Dad money and had promised to pay him back before the year was out, and it was now near mid-December.

"If it was the money," Mother wondered, "why couldn't someone else watch over Effie while Ed came to deliver it himself?"

"Or," Dad said, "he could have sent the money with Randy."

At that point in the conversation, they both broke out laughing at the same time, knowing that Ed could not trust his younger brother with anything, not Effie, and especially not money.

"I'll go tomorrow," Dad said.

The Renfrows were distant relatives, as Ed had married Dad's second cousin Effie, but we seldom ever saw them. They lived in a backwoods area remote from our own farm and both Dad and Mother agreed they were good but rough people, and the brother, Randy, had the reputation of being shiftless and unreliable. In deciding to go, Dad hoped out loud that he was getting his money back, and I was silently hoping he would take me along with him. I had just turned five at the time and wasn't sure my mom would allow me out in the cold for an entire day, but Dad then said,

"Son, you'll be coming with me."

In the early dark of the next morning, Mother layered me with clothing against the cold while Dad saddled Anthony, his oldest and gentlest mule, and brought him to our front porch. Well, "saddled" might not be the right term as it wasn't a real one, just a padded leather patch with a girth hitch, devised by Dad. He lifted me onto the mule, then mounted behind me, saying,

"We'll be home by dark."

Mother handed up a neck-bag containing sausage-and-biscuit sandwiches and a bottle of water for snacks, and a quart jar of Dad's freshest sorghum molasses for Effie. The neck-bag, another of Dad's creations, was a two-part bag like a saddlebag, except it slings over the neck of the mule in front of the rider. Dad had stitched it together from cotton-sack canvas and used it when traveling by mule.

As we started our trek, the road, powdered with snow from the previous day's fall, was frozen firm, and we would have no problem with mud. I pulled my scarf higher to protect my numbed cheeks from the freezing cold. I could smell the pork sausage in the neck-bag, and the familiar odor of mule drifted up as the animal warmed with walking—a mix of skin and hair smells, with a slight whiff of manure. Odors seemed more separate and precise in the dry cold.

After riding through the sunrise, the plowed fields and meadows gave way to thicker forest cover, and a light snow started floating from the sky. There was no wind, and in the cold and silent morning, we heard only the muffled clip-clop of Anthony's hooves as the snowfall increased. After passing a bare oak filled with clamoring crows, we crunched our way through an ice-crusted stream and climbed a hill, where the leafless trees faded quickly into evergreen conifers as the snowfall continued.

"I hope we don't get snowed–in down here," Dad said. "Don't want to spend all that much time with the Renfrows."

I asked Dad why there were no cleared fields, and he explained that folks in this neck of the woods were more trappers, hunters, and gatherers.

"They live off the land in a different way than we do," he said.

As we rode, Dad explained more about the way the Renfrows lived, hunting and trapping animals for food and pelts, running trotlines in the river for fish, keeping a small kitchen garden, and sometimes working at a timber harvest or road maintenance job. They tanned their own animal hides and even made their own whisky. I guessed to myself that Randy was the whisky man in the family. I learned later that Effie's family, the branch related to Dad, had prevailed on him to help the Renfrows get started in tobacco farming. Dad had agreed to provide planting advice and a small loan for their first crop, which had, by then, already been harvested and sold at the tobacco auction.

After traveling for what seemed like a long distance, Dad was now looking for the connection to a smaller road that would take us to the Renfrow homestead. With so much snow, he couldn't recognize the turn and hoped he hadn't missed it. I felt sure he hadn't, knowing he never got lost, and was always ready to give directions to any traveler.

With the snowfall increasing, we stopped for him to ponder and have a drink of water. After a long pause and some very serious thought on whether to go forward or turn back, Dad set us off again in the same direction down the road. After a short while, we heard the muffled sounds of a horse up ahead, and a dark image slowly appeared through the white haze of the falling snow. A fur-bundled man approached driving a one-horse sled with sideboards. Dad asked: "Is Ed Renfrow's house further down the road?"

"Yes sir, another furlong down," he said. "There's an iron post at the turn. Don't miss it, 'case you can't see the side road in this snow."

As the fur-man drove on, I saw a deer carcass, dripping blood, in the back of his sled—a four-pointer.

We found the post at the turn and saw traces of smoke in the sky above the trees as we rode downhill toward a sizeable log house on a flat area near the river. At the end of the house nearest us was a fieldstone chimney with two arched shelters built into its sloping sides. As we approached, two scruffy hounds erupted from the chimney openings and ran barking and snarling around the mule. We stopped near the house and waited for Ed Renfrow to come out and call off the dogs before dismounting.

It took a while, but he finally appeared and welcomed us from his porch, calling to the dogs which circled at a respectful distance as we dismounted, then returned to their openings in the chimney wall. We walked past a snow-covered pile of long, thin logs, and onto the porch. Dad and Renfrow shook hands, and Dad, tilting his head toward me, said: "This is my boy."

Stepping around a long log on the porch, we entered a large room with the fireplace at one end and a bed at the other, and a door to what must have been a bedroom. In the winter, they probably used only one room for both living and sleeping. Effie, a cheerful woman with dark hair and a pale face, sitting propped-up in the bed, greeted us with a smile. Dad set the jar of molasses on the dresser next to the bed.

"This was a good year for my sorghum—brought you some of the best."

She thanked him, and after some conversation about family, we un-layered our wraps.

Renfrow, a stocky man with red hair and a reddish face, asked us to sit with him facing the fire. The chairs he offered looked handmade of wood, with the seat and back webbing of deer-hide strips with the hair still on them. What caught my attention when we first entered the room was the fireplace. Made of fieldstone with clay mortar, it had a big opening with a roaring fire, but instead of having cut wood in the firebox, a log was being fed into the fireplace, with most of it still extending out into the room, right there on the floor. I had never seen such a thing but was reminded of the illustrations I'd seen in books depicting the bringing in of the Yule log for Christmas celebrations. In the book, kids rode the decorated log as it was dragged from the field to the fireplace then fed end-first into the fire to burn as the celebrants drank hot punch dipped from a big bowl. This was no celebration here, but a similar idea. There was no hot punch either, but later we each got a pickled egg and a glass of spring water. Dad was offered whisky but declined.

As the conversation went to weather and then business, Renfrow handed Dad a small, twine-bound bundle of money.

"I'm much obliged to you for the loan, much obliged," he said.

Our host then, with a small grunt, shoved the log further into the fire. As the conversation continued, the dogs suddenly started barking as if under attack. I thought more visitors had arrived, but Renfrow made no move to respond, only commenting that one dog was smarter than the other. He then explained that one of the cubby holes in the outside of the chimney was warmer than the other. After our arrival, the mistrustful smart dog stayed near us longer, and the other got the warm cubby. After getting a bit chilled, the smart one ran barking out toward the road as if visitors were there, drawing the other out to bark with him. The smart dog then ran back and took the warm cubby.

"That dumb dog never will learn that trick, but he can tree a squirrel real good," Renfrow explained. "The smart one," he smiled, "reminds me of a politician I use'ta know."

Effie asked us to stay for dinner, but Dad said we had to get back while there was still enough light; said he couldn't make his way in the snow just by the moon shine. Renfrow walked us out to the porch and kept the dogs quiet. They circled us as we mounted the mule, and watched as we rode up the steep slope. It had stopped snowing, but the cover was much thicker than when we came, and the air seemed even colder than before. Anthony slipped some at the bottom but found his footing as the slope flattened.

"We'll make it home just fine," Dad said. "Renfrow is too lazy to chop firewood, but someway got the money. I'm real glad to get my money back." He then added: "I'm glad too that the dogs didn't get our biscuits and sausage."

Some distance away as I was handing Dad a biscuit, we heard ferocious barking in the distance down the hill behind us. We both smiled, knowing which dog would get the warm cubby, and that Renfrow had yet another long log waiting on the porch to be fed into his fire.

During the ride home, I told Dad how the long log in the fireplace reminded me of the Yule logs described and pictured in book illustrations. We also talked about Renfrow's dogs. I told Dad:

"If we decide to get us a dog, it ought to be a smart one."

Dad agreed, of course. I hadn't yet asked for a dog, but the subject was now open for discussion, so I brought up my next subject.

"Don't you think we could have us a Yule log and punch bowl this Christmas?"

"A wassail bowl," Dad said. "Good idea. We can do the bowl easy enough, but I doubt your mom would want a rough log and loose bark scratching up her floor. We'll just have to make the Yule small enough to fit in our fireplace."

I was a cold but happy boy. I really wanted to have a puppy, and the Yule log and wassail bowl would be nice too. *Who knows*, I thought. *I might get a smart dog for Christmas, and it's only three weeks away.*

THE BARLOW

A Barlow pocket knife, the first gift I remember receiving from my dad, introduced me to an exciting boyhood. I was five years old when he surprised me with it and insisted on telling me a cautionary tale about his own first knife, also a Barlow, and how he'd lost it.

A month or so after he had received his knife, Dad was out roaming the countryside with a pal, as he often did, when it began to rain. They took shelter in a farmer's cotton crib, a roofed structure with spaced timber sides, used to store cotton until enough had been picked for a load to the gin. When they jumped into the crib, the cotton was soft and fluffy, and for fun, they leapt repeatedly from the side rails, and rough-housed and wrestled on the cotton until the rain stopped. When they left the crib, the cotton had been packed down to a fraction of its previous volume, which the boys paid no notice of. Upon arriving home, he noticed his knife was missing. He didn't know where he had lost it but reasoned that it must have been in the cotton crib. If he had gone back to the crib—a long distance away— he didn't think he would find it among the clumps of cotton. It was given him by his granddad, and he didn't dare to tell his granddad he'd lost it.

On a Saturday soon after, Dad went to town with his family for trade day. Walking around on his own looking for another boy to play with, he walked into a small group of farmers, one of whom was breaking the news that there was a cotton thief somewhere in the township who had stolen most of his stored cotton. He then held up Dad's pocket knife, saying the thief had dropped it at the crime scene, and asked if anyone knew who owned it. If Dad had claimed his knife, he would have been branded as the thief, with serious consequences as the farmer was convinced his cotton had been stolen. Dad, of course, didn't claim the knife, and eventually told his granddad how he'd lost it. It took him quite some time to get another to replace it.

After his story, Dad introduced me to the use and care of my knife.

"Don't ever lose your knife, son. Keep it with you wherever you go, except maybe when going to church. I'll teach you how to keep it sharp, and you have to be careful and not cut yourself. This is the whetstone you'll use to sharpen it."

He produced a whetstone about four inches long, added some oil, and started rubbing the blade on the stone in circular motions. After sharpening one side of the blade, he had me sharpen the other.

With the knife sharpened, he said: "Now let's go and make something," and the fun began.

He led me to a growth of young hickory bushes along the stream bed of the branch just down the hill from our house and downstream from the spring house. Hickory has unusual qualities; it's soft and very pliable when green, and very dense, fine-grained, and hard when cured, making it a favorite for ax and hammer handles. Hickory's loose, slick bark attaches to its wood core with a viscous sap, making it useful for whistles. Dad cut a hickory twig about a half-inch in diameter and four inches long, then cut a crosswise, V-shaped groove an inch or so from one end. He slid the tube of bark back from the wood core and cut a horizontal channel along the top of the wood from the V-groove to the short end, which was then cross-cut at 45 degrees for a mouthpiece. Sliding the wood core back into the bark tube completed the whistle, which made a very nice sound. He explained the sound could change, high or low, depending on its length and where the cross-groove was cut. He helped me carve another similar whistle with slightly different dimensions that produced a higher pitch.

Next, we built a waterwheel. From a young hickory bush, he cut a straight stick about six inches long for a wheel axle and two Y-shaped sticks from the same limb for supports. Finding a narrow, swift water passage in the branch, he sharpened the Y-shaped twigs at the bottom and had me push them into the mud of the stream, leaving the forks to support the axle of the wheel. Having carved flat paddle blades from another twig, he made lengthwise slits in the pliable but tough bark of the axle and pushed the two paddles halfway through the slits making a wheel with four evenly spaced paddles, which spun very nicely in the narrow, rushing stream.

We left the water wheel spinning as he started cutting the stock for a slingshot. From a three-quarter-inch-thick fork of a green hickory twig, he cut a Y-shaped stock about six inches high and cut grooves around the tips of the "Y" where rubber bands were to be connected.

"We'll have to finish this at home," he said, "but we have a good stout stock to start with."

In his workshop under the house, he cut part of an old rubber tire inner tube into two strips about one-half inch wide and eight inches long, looped them over the top of the "Y" ends of the stock, and tied them on with twine. The other ends of the rubber strips were pushed through vertical slits in an oval-shaped piece of leather, folded and tied back onto themselves with twine, making a pouch for holding the pebbles to be shot. A few tries told us that his fabrication was a success. His next admonishment was,

"Be careful with this, and don't shoot anybody. A stone from this could put an eye out, so no slingshot fights with other boys."

Now in possession of a pocket knife, a whistle, and a slingshot as new tools, I was ready to deal with the wonderful countryside world around me. From that day forward, I usually carried my Barlow in my right front pocket, my slingshot in my right hip pocket, and shot-sized pebbles in my other front pocket.

While I felt ready for almost anything with my new tools, I soon learned more about the reality of the woods. My parents and Grandma had given me strong warnings of the many dangers in the surrounding woods, poisonous snakes being the primary hazard. I learned that copperheads are aggressive and hang out among rocks, and that I could expect to encounter water moccasins in just about any stream bed or in its surrounding vegetation. Then in one instance, I came dangerously close to a copperhead by relying too much on my slingshot, thinking I could kill him with it. I escaped un-bitten but realized I couldn't reliably kill snakes with it and started carrying a snake-stick, or staff, as well as the slingshot when out roaming.

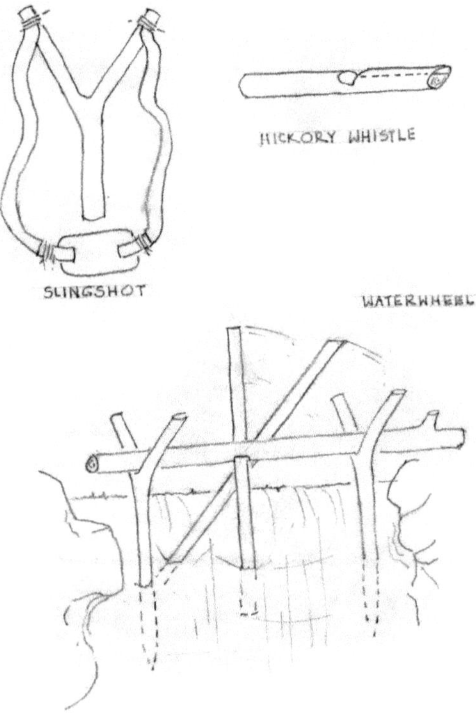

BOYS OF THE WILD

Soon after the Barlow came into my life, I met a boy named "Junior" from a nearby farm when he came over one day with his dad. Our dads went off to check the crops, leaving us together on the front porch. He was a thin boy with light-brown hair, blue eyes, and a spatter of freckles across the bridge of his nose. His ears stuck out a little too far, but that may have been because of a bad haircut, clipped too close at the sides. When he saw me looking at his haircut, he said:

"Bad haircut. I know. Don't ever let your mama cut your hair when she's mad. You hav'ta go hide."

Mother joined us as I was showing him my new Barlow. He greeted Mother with a proper "Maam," and continued closely examining the knife.

"This is a real good one," he declared. "I've done lost the one I had, but it warn't worth a fart in a whirlwind anyways."

This was language Mother would never have tolerated from me, but with the edge of a smile on her face, I could tell she liked this somewhat crude but charming boy as much as I did. He had a dog whose whole name was Rufus Rastus Johnson Brown, but everybody just called him Rufus. Junior and I, along with Rufus, began roaming the fields, woods, and streams around our farms. Although a year younger than I, Junior taught me things I didn't know about our surroundings. I was also a "Junior," and we were so often together, Mother called us "the Juniors." Grandma Elizabeth, who also gave us advice on snakes and especially on poisonous plants, referred to the two of us as the "boys of the wild."

When crossing a backroad, we could smell gasoline exhaust if a car had been through in the past hour or so. With some practice, our senses became well-tuned. We were good at visually spotting wildlife and could often smell a snake before we saw it. Nonetheless, Rufus detected snakes quicker than we could, and we were glad to have him along.

We learned to judge hickory trees by size as to whether we could ride them down. This sport involved climbing high enough up a hickory that our weight caused the flexible tree to bend down and let us step off onto the ground. If the tree was too big for our weight, unable to bend it sufficiently, we had to climb back down. Terrapins were always an interesting find, with their diamond-patterned shell and yellow belly. When we lifted them off the ground, we liked to hear the gushing air sound they made as they retreated inside their shells. We also liked catching toads but were careful when picking them up. We were told that if they peed on our hands, it would cause warts.

Junior and I pursued muscadines and peckerwoods, two of the things in the woods we enjoyed most, using the technique of triangulation. Hearing a peckerwood, we would stop, say nothing, and move away from each other for a considerable distance, each of us then following the sound to its source, and our paths would converge at a point very close to the bird's location. Using stealth, we would get as close to him as possible to see his bright colors and watch him at his work picking grubs and bugs from the bark.

Muscadines, a very aromatic wild grape, produced a treat whenever we could find them. When we smelled a patch of them, we would triangulate by their sweet, musky odor, moving away from each other and checking whether the odor increased or decreased in intensity as we moved. Muscadine vines climb trees and are hard to spot visually, but our odor triangulation worked every time. Shaking the vines causes the ripe ones to fall, but often we had to climb for them. After finding the grapes, we would play a game of mumblety-peg and the loser would climb the tree and vines to pick our sweet bounty and drop it down to the other. We were both winners when muscadines were found. We sometimes brought home muscadines or crawdads, but after I brought home a toad in my pocket, Mother asked us not to bring anything home, even though I explained I'd washed him in the branch before putting him in my pocket.

In the summer seasons later on, Junior and I added electric fences to our adventures. After electrification came to Cleburne County, farmers started installing electric fences, consisting of a single bare wire connected to wooden posts with ceramic insulators. Discovering one, we heard the fence before we saw it, as it operated from a box that made a loud click every few seconds as it fired, sending an electric surge through the fence wires. I hadn't seen one before, but Junior knew about them. He told me I would get a hefty shock if I touched the electrified fence wire with my fingers but showed me how we could grab the fence wire with our fists without getting hurt. I was reluctant, afraid of being shocked, but he gave me a hands-on demonstration. He had me touch the wire with my finger, which stung sharply, with a spark hitting my finger before I even touched the wire. Then he grabbed the hot wire with his fist, held on, and had me do the same. The current surged through our arms without hurting. We would grab the wire in both our clinched fists and hold while the alternating electrical charges pulsed through our arms causing our arm muscles to contract with each jolt, both yelling: " Yahoo!" We called it "The Thrill of the Wild."

Looking back on my boyhood activities there, I'm surprised I was never bitten by snakes, as I was so often among them. One day when Junior and I were going crawdad fishing, I convinced Mother that we should build a fire to cook and eat our catch fresh there on the stream bank. We left my house with a heavy iron skillet, some lard, and in my pocket, a handful of kitchen matches. I felt proud and well-equipped with the skillet hanging from my belt, but soon learned I couldn't walk with it dangling against my legs, so I held it in one hand and my snake stick in the other. Our plan was to fish the shallow area upstream of the deepest part of the branch, which we called our swimming hole. As we reached the swimming hole, we noticed a large, cottonmouth water moccasin resting on a hickory branch above and watched as it dropped into the water where we had swum the day before. As we watched it swim away, our appetite for sautéed crawdad also disappeared.

"Let's not swim here any longer," I told Junior.

"And," Junior said, "let's not grapple for crawdads today."

On our way back home, we even gave wide berth to the rock outcropping we knew was crawling with copperheads, and where I had already killed two in the path we walked.

BETTIS SCHOOL

The Bettis family, whose farmstead we leased, had initially migrated from South Carolina to what is now Cleburne County, Arkansas, in the 1850s, and settled on the land the family held four miles northeast of the town of Quitman. Bringing their fundamentalist religion with them, they founded the Nazareth Cumberland Presbyterian Church in 1878. Some years later, James Bettis—or Jimmy as my parents called him —donated a square-acre parcel of their land holdings for the construction in 1904 of a new church. The church, built with donated materials and labor, also served as the Bettis Community School. After the church disbanded many years later, the Bettis School endured, ready and waiting for my first school experience.

It was late August when Mother met the new teacher who was to commence the next school year in early September. At five years old, I was not yet of school age, as my birthday was late in the year— November. Mother and the teacher, however, had a meeting of the minds as the teacher herself had a daughter who would not be six until December. She had intended to bring her daughter to school anyway, not knowing what else to do with her each day when she went off to teach. When she agreed to take me into school early along with her daughter, my parents, both big on education, welcomed the opportunity of giving me a head-start. I also suspect Mother relished the chance to get me out of the house and off the farm for at least part of each day, somewhat easing her daily life, which then included the care of my infant brother, Alder Lee. My companion, Junior, was younger than I and not yet ready to attend, nor would any of my cousins, most all of whom lived in the McAnear School attendance area some miles away. I wouldn't know a single pupil at the school, but that didn't matter to me.

Going to school was a new adventure for me, and each new thing I learned left quite an impression. On the first day of school, Mother gave me a dinner of biscuit-and-ham sandwiches and a baked sweet potato, all wrapped in newspaper and tied with twine. She also included milk in a screw-top bottle that once contained vinegar. School started, or "books took up" as we then said, at 8:30 so I was sent off at the proper time to be there early for registration.

The walk to school was a short one. Our house was built facing a rural road, already abandoned at that time for a new county road at the other side of the property. The same abandoned road continued past our house, across a stream branch, and up the hill past the Bettis School. The long-abandoned bridge crossing the branch on the old road still had its support beams in place, but the deck structure was a splintering of 4' x 8' timber remnants, with rusty iron spikes protruding from the support beams, and no longer a safe crossing. Instead of crossing at branch level to get to school, I chose to take the ruined bridge anyway, selected a beam to walk and, at risk of slipping and falling, made my way across. I tested my balance and skill by walking the beam foot-in-front-of-foot, the way I was told the Osage Indians had walked these hills and forests in times before us. The old bridge, being some twelve feet above the water, was much more exciting than fording the branch or crossing on a felled log further upstream. After my first day of school, I later selected the easiest beam to walk and made that my usual crossing route to and from school. After registration and that first day of school, I quickly fell into, and enjoyed, the routine of attending classes.

* * * * *

The schoolhouse, a board-and-batten, wood frame structure, was built on the hill that sloped down to the old road. We climbed stairs to the entry of the one-room structure, which had chairs and benches for seating, and a large iron heating stove near the center of the room. The older children sat in the back and the younger in front. The teacher rotated groups of students to the front row when it was time to teach that grade. Then they were moved back to their seats to study quietly while another group moved to the front row for their lesson. Discipline was strict, and everyone had to study and keep quiet as each grade seated itself in the front row for its lessons and recitations. I quickly learned to answer "present" when named in roll call, and to stand when called on by the teacher. On Fridays, we had orthography and an occasional spelling bee, neither of which I was good at.

The older boys hauled drinking water in a bucket from the branch and in winter, also hauled in the donated firewood, which was stored under the schoolhouse. The water bucket had a tin dipper hanging from its rim, which we all shared when getting a drink. We weren't allowed to drink while classes were in session, so at break time we all went to the water bucket, and one at a time, we passed the dipper to the next person as we had our drink. When turnip greens were in season, the teacher would bring them from her garden, cook them up on the heating stove, and feed the kids who wanted some. Most of us just ate the lunch we had brought.

My new situation of being with older children appealed to me, especially being with the boys who seemed to know so much more than I did. I sat as close as I could to whichever class was being held at the front row to see what the older kids were studying. If and when they would let us, we younger kids could also play with the older ones at lunch hour and during the morning and afternoon recesses. I thought our teacher was very smart and kind in the way she kept good order in the classroom. I think all the kids liked her.

I hadn't been with so many kids before, and during warm weather, looking at everyone's bare arms, I realized that every boy and girl had the same smallpox vaccination scar on their upper-left arm just below the shoulder. I had thought I and some of my cousins were the only ones with the scar.

Also during warm weather, when we arrived at school each day, we took our milk bottles to the branch down the hill from the school, tied strings to the necks, and lowered them into a deep part of the stream to keep them cool. The array of bottles in the water displayed all shapes and sizes, depending on what sealable container each family happened to have. Some kids brought their lunches in half-gallon lard pails, and others, like me, wrapped in newspaper and tied with twine, or in a brown paper poke. I'm sure Mother knew I would forget a pail at least once or twice a week and wanted to save them for other uses. Those who used pails probably had tougher mothers, who threatened something like disembowelment for a forgotten pail. Discipline started earlier with some than with others, but I still got my share of it, both at school and at home.

The schoolyard play area was problematic, as the entire site was on a slope too steep and rocky for use as a playing field. We tried baseball games when one boy brought a baseball he'd made from a ball of odd lengths of twine wrapped with surgical tape, and a home-made oak bat. We played a few times by going off the schoolyard to Dad's adjacent sorghum patch, which was much flatter, but it could only be used when there was no crop. Because of its soft soil, it was also a favorite place for mumblety-peg, a game we played with a jack knife with folding blades, a device every schoolboy carried in his pocket. We also played "King of the Hill" a few times on the mounds of soil Dad left from a potato crop, but field games were, for the most part, impractical. A game of crack the whip (a traditional outdoor game with linked hands in a moving line like a whip) in the schoolyard was interrupted by the teacher, who deemed it too dangerous for the rocky slope, especially for the young girls, who might get hurled into the rocks if they ended up at the tip of the whip.

One day an older boy named Randall, who had many ideas about many things, got the boys together to build a flying jinny—a primitive version of a carousel. At that point, the jinny was the most exciting undertaking at the school, play-wise. Three of the older boys brought tools to school one day, and we all helped with the construction. Randall brought a two-handled, cross-cut lumberman's saw over his shoulder, which sprang and bounced with each step he took. Others brought tools such as a handsaw, augers for drilling, and a drawing knife for peeling bark from freshly cut poles. Our team selected an oak tree in the schoolyard, about five inches in diameter, and sawed it off about four feet above the ground. The cut area of the stump was shaped to slope slightly from center down to the outer bark to form the base post. A smaller pine of four or so inches in diameter and some twelve feet long, was cut down and its bark peeled to serve as a beam. We balanced the beam on the stump, drilled a hole in the beam, and drove a long bolt into the stump to hold the beam in place and serve as the axle. My job in the process was to hold one end of the beam as it was being balanced on the stump for the hole and bolt. The hole in the beam was made big enough for it to spin freely making a simple flying jinny. Another boy, whose dad repaired tractors and farm implements as a side job, brought three big washers to school to improve our jinny. We helped him remove the pin and replace it, adding two washers on the bottom and one on top of the beam, all slathered with axle grease, to improve its performance and make it last longer.

"Now it goes like greased lightning," he said proudly.

We would start pushing the beam standing on the higher slope, and jump on, riding on our stomachs around the lower slope where our feet couldn't reach the ground. Other kids kept the beam spinning while two riders at a time, one on each end, took turns on the beam.

During this time, I was the proud recipient of a leather aviator's helmet as a hand-me-down from an older boy in our extended family. I was disappointed, however, that it didn't come with the aviator's goggles, which were usually paired-up with it. I liked it anyhow, and was fond of wearing it on the jinny, pretending to be a pilot flying through the sky. Every pupil at the school rode the jinny every day, it seemed. We rode it and rode it and rode it, until we were all turngiddy.

Since all the other kids were older, I was learning a lot from them. They all lived on farms and were familiar with animals, but one boy was something of an encyclopedia of animal husbandry. In an argument with another boy on how particular animals defecate, he gave us all what I now recognize as a "seminar" on the subject. Contorting his body into a convincing semblance of whichever animal he was depicting, he would go through the entire process, even describing what the manure looked like at the end of each demonstration. For the goat, which most of us weren't very familiar with, he carefully collected pebbles of the correct size, and holding the handful to his own behind, dropped them in carefully patterned and timed bunches, as he told us the goat would. From that day forward, he was recognized as the school's expert on animals and could even describe for us—and draw pictures of—exotic animals living in faraway parts of the world. Randall, our idea man, seemed to know many things the rest of us didn't and was also our best help on what I would now call "sexology."

Other practical things I was learning were swear words and naughty words, and what the difference was between them. This got me into trouble, as I hadn't yet learned not to use them in front of adults. Our teacher heard me spouting four-letter words, none of which I knew the meaning of, and promptly sent me home. I left the school, and at the ruined bridge, stopped to ponder my situation. I had been walking the ragged bridge beams every school day since my first, yet crossing it to go home that day seemed harder than overcoming my fear at my first crossing. I had to decide whether to return home and face the wrath of my mother or disappear into the woods until school was out and go home at the usual time. The latter seemed the clever thing to do, but I knew that my teacher and Mother talked to each other often, and I would be the subject of their next conversation. So, again I walked the beam and dallying here and dallying there, moped my way home.

At home, Mother was in her usual pattern of the day: ironing and listening to soap operas on the radio. Before starting school, I'd learned she began her day early with whatever housework or chores required moving about the house or in the garden, and saved sewing and ironing for the afternoon radio programs. Her favorite ones were *Just Plain Bill, Stella Dallas, Backstage Wife*, and *Portia Faces Life*. She was right in the middle of Stella Dallas when I arrived.

"What are you doing home at this hour?" the query came.

"I was sent home," I said, making it as simple as possible.

"What for?" was, of course, the next question.

"For saying a bad word," I replied, not disclosing there had been a whole string of them.

"I don't want to hear you say it," she said, and produced a scrap of paper and a pencil for me to write it down. I wrote a four-letter word in capitals and returned the paper. She glanced at it and dropped it into the fireplace, where it disappeared in a yellow puff of flame.

"You're in trouble, mister. Shame on your face!" she said. "Go to your room and study your lessons until your dad comes home. He'll decide what to do with you."

I had the feeling she was more annoyed at me for disturbing her soap opera than for having said a naughty word. I was referred to Dad, who later took me for a walk and gave me a reprimand, along with some conflicting advice.

"You are not to say such words again. It's important you stay in school and not be sent home." He then added, "And be careful where you are and who might be listening when you use bad language."

* * * * *

Another advantage of being in school with older kids was sex education, or at least some semblance of it. In the schoolyard, there was an oak, which the older boys started calling the "pussy tree." The tree had lost a limb a few feet above the ground, probably in an ice storm that produced more weight than the limb could bear. The elongated vertical scar had partially re-grown around the edges, producing what looked like inner and outer labia with a deep indentation in the middle, the whole of which resembled a vulva. I was amazed to learn what the scar looked like, and I think the other boys were as well. It seemed Randall was the only one who knew what one looked like, but he had all the boys making what sounded like knowledgeable comments on the phenomenon. An enlightening, practical demonstration was performed during afternoon recess one day by, yet again, Randall, my senior mentor.

Randall had found a fallen pine limb in the nearby woods that looked like a large penis, with the end where it broke from the tree looking very much like the head of one. The size seemed right for the pussy tree, and he broke off the other end at the right length to hold the limb between his legs and simulate a sex act with the desired tree. He gathered us boys at the tree, and with all standing round, straddled the limb and holding it with both hands, started his performance, rubbing the head end of the limb in the scar of the tree, and making thrusting motions with his hips. Very soon, the girls started appearing and, seemingly inspired by the bigger audience, he began to include running thrusts at his target with the limb still held between his legs. The entire school of kids was standing in a large circle, stunned to silence by his performance, when the teacher saw what was happening. She ran down the steps shouting for our star performer to stop, and at all the rest of us for being an audience. She declared the recess over, sending us back up to the schoolhouse where, hopping mad, she gave us a lecture, the contents of which I don't remember. Randall was then singled out for her sterner reprimand, taking him outside for its delivery. She returned without Randall, and I wasn't clear at the time whether she had killed him, sent him home, or if he had fled the scene. I was never sure whether or not she told my mother about the event, but my naughty word transgression seemed pale in comparison to Randall's spectacular, and for the kids, enlightening performance.

Looking back on the event, I realize our teacher must have feared for her job and had to respond as expected of her. But with some presence of mind, looking down the eight or so schoolhouse steps and further down the slope of the hill, she might have seen a large oak at the very edge of a circle formed by diminutive, tree-worshipping Druids silently performing an obscene ritual, perhaps a celebration to herald the coming of spring. She might have simply said: "Welcome, spring," and allowed the performance to continue.

The one-room Bettis School, simple as it was, was a good beginning for my education, acculturation, and introduction to the wonders of the world beyond the woods, meadows, and streams I had already embraced as my own. I'm thankful to the Bettis family for founding, contributing to, and maintaining the school. But for the religious fervor of the original Bettis bunch who organized a new church and built the church-schoolhouse, I would not have had this unique opportunity. So, despite some reluctance to do so, I guess I should also thank God.

THE GREEN DODGE

Ol' Shimmy-Shack

Just home from school on a late spring afternoon, I was ready for the best part of the day, wandering the farmstead creeks and thickets with my slingshot in one pocket and my Barlow knife in the other. Mom told me that Dad had gone to Heber Springs with a neighbor and should be back soon, so I took the branch streamed and walked down to where our farm road connected to the county road, hoping to meet up with him there. As I neared the road, I heard a car engine racing and came out of the thicket to find Dad sitting in the driver's seat of a green sedan stuck in the mud. There was no culvert where our farm road joined to the county road, only a muddy swale, which seemed to be swallowing the hindquarters of the car. In his annoyance and unfamiliarity with the vehicle just purchased, he had flooded the engine, as he later admitted. Billows of blue smoke hung over the mud and spinning wheels. When I arrived, he shut off the engine and told me,

"I've bought us a car, Sonny Boy. You can help me get it up the hill."

I thought I would be having to push, but he said: "You sit here in the driver's seat, and I'll get a mule to pull us out of this slop."

While he was gone to fetch the mule, I sat grasping the varnished, hardwood steering wheel, surprised how my afternoon was turning out. The car had green leather seats stitched into rolls, which looked quite fancy. It had a dome light over the rear seat, and the ceiling was padded with a fuzzy fabric. It even had a windshield wiper operated by a little hand crank above the windshield. The exhaust smoke hung heavy in the air, but I could still smell the fine leather seats. I sat too low to see out through the windshield, but just knew I would be driving it soon.

Dad re-appeared with Amos and hooked the mule's trace chains to the car's front bumper at the two places where it bolted to the frame.

"Hold the steering wheel tight so the front wheels stay straight. Amos will pull us out." Dad held the reins of the mule as he urged him through the heavy pull. Amos strained to get the car moving, then slowly eased it out until all four wheels were on firm ground as I furiously held the steering wheel in position. With the trace chains stowed in the floor of the back seat, Dad tethered Amos to the rear bumper with a rope.

"You watch Amos from the back seat to see if he can follow along. I'll try to drive slow."

Kneeling on the back seat and looking out the rear window, I gave a running report on Amos. He cantered along and had to gallop only once.

Our arrival at the house was something like a homecoming. Mother was there holding my infant brother Alder Lee and looked surprised we'd arrived in a car and towing a mule behind it. Sis came out, and along with Dad, me, and Amos, we all stood in a semi-circle looking at the car. Dad made the introduction, holding the mule's reins with one hand and gesturing with the other.

"It's a 1929 Dodge Brothers with a six-cylinder engine, and it's a four-door sedan with room for the whole family."

I thought it looked wonderful, painted a rich, dark green with shiny black fenders, yellow pin-stripes front-to-back along the body, and wood-spoked wheels painted the same yellow as the stripes. Big headlights were mounted on a bar between the fenders at the front, and smaller lights mounted on each side of the body in front of the front doors.

Mother loved the car and was glad to have it. She and Dad had often talked about getting a used car, and this one looked better than she expected. Twelve-year-old Sis was already counting how many of her friends would fit in the back seat with her. I noticed that Amos was looking at the car too, with his head turned a little to one side. Dad once told me that mules are pretty smart, and I wondered what Amos might be thinking. He was probably wondering if he would have to pull this thing around from now on, or maybe canter along tied behind it.

After the introduction, Dad said: "We're lucky to have such a fine car in this wartime world. Let me take us for a ride."

We all got in, 'cept for Amos, of course, and Dad drove us down the farm road, turned around near the mud patch, and drove back up to the house. As he turned it around, he said: "I'll have to think some about how to get it through that muddy ditch."

It was, in fact, wartime, as Dad said, and many items were becoming scarce, especially those containing steel or rubber. There was even talk in the newspaper that food, gasoline, and many other items and commodities might soon be rationed. He knew the car would soon need new tires, which were already scarce. While driving the car home from Heber Springs, he had noticed a bad shimmy in the steering mechanism and was worried about getting replacement parts, also a wartime scarcity.

A few days later, Dad repaired the muddy swale. I wasn't old enough to be of help but watched as he laid two logs parallel along the bottom of the swale, spaced so water could flow between. He then placed another log on top of the two and covered them with earth fill so the car could drive over the surface without a bump.

With the drainage swale repaired, the next morning Dad took us driving on the county road to get used to how the car operated. After several car-lengths of travel, the badly worn steering caused the front wheels to shimmy. To break the shimmy, Dad yanked the steering wheel to one side and shouted, "Cut it out!" We helped him by chanting "shimmy-shack, shimmy-shack, cut it out!" several times when it happened, so Dad didn't have to say it. The name of the Dodge was "Ol' Shimmy-Shack" from then on.

Another problem with the car was a badly worn fuel pump. The pump, connected to and operated by the engine, forced fuel from the tank at the back to the carburetor on the engine at the front. The weak pump worked fine on level roads, but when climbing a hill, gravity kicked in, and it could no longer lift fuel from the lower tank to the much higher engine, and the fuel-starved engine would stall. If a hill became too steep and the engine began to stall, Dad would stop and let the car roll backwards down the hill, trying all the while to keep the engine running. At the bottom of the hill, he would turn the car around and back it up the hill in reverse. With gravity's help, the engine could get fuel, and the car drove uphill just fine in reverse. Dad soon learned to guess the slope of any upcoming hill and determine whether the car could make the climb without stalling. For the steepest hills, those he called "backup hills," he would turn the car around and start the climb in reverse gear at the very bottom and back it up the hill. After each backup climb, we would all give Dad and the car a big cheer as we reached the top.

The mechanic at the garage in Heber Springs told Dad the shimmy was caused by worn-out tie-rod bushings in the steering gear linkage. I memorized the term but had trouble understanding what it meant, so with both our heads under a front fender, Dad showed me the defective parts. After a couple of months, the mechanic got the parts and installed them. He couldn't get a replacement fuel pump, so Dad continued backing up hills.

* * * * *

In the fall of the year with crops laid by, our folks were discussing a trip to Stone County for a visit with Dad's uncle John Coe, someone he hadn't seen in years.

"And now that we have a car," Dad said, "why not?"

Why not? Stone County, where the Coes lived, is a hilly country, and Mother and Dad were discussing how much of the trip would be uphill. Dad still hadn't found a fuel pump, but by then had become rather good at driving backwards up steep hills.

"Those hills may be longer and steeper than you reckon," Mother said.

Dad agreed, and added: "Reverse gear is slower than the other gears, so it'll take a longer while to get there."

Mother and Dad continued their discussion as I was sent to bed, but at breakfast the next morning I learned they had decided Ol' Shimmy-Shack could make it, and we would take the trip.

A week or so later, we left at daybreak with a full tank of gas, luggage strapped to the back of the car, and a stuffed lunch basket on the back seat between Sis and me. I wore a new pair of green corduroy britches with a matching jacket Mother had bought me, which I thought must have been special made to wear in the green car. Sis wore a prissy new dress Mother had sewn for her the week before, and in Mother's arms, infant Alder Lee was so bundled up in wraps you couldn't tell there was a kid in there. In the optimism of the bright fall morning, we declared ourselves in good spirits and ready for our trip. We were off to Stone County in the Green Dodge, on our first of many family outings in Ol' Shimmy-Shack.

"We'll be there by sundown," Dad said, "if nothing bends nor breaks."

The first part of our trip seemed easy, with a few backup hills along the way, but something did break. I was already schooled on one set of car parts—tie-rod bushings—but soon learned another: the timer chain. The chain, which tells the spark plugs when to fire, was too slack and jumped a few cogs, causing the car to sputter, pop, and barely move. Dad slowly limped the stuttering car some miles to the town of Mountain View where we arrived just as darkness fell. He found a mechanic who re-opened his closed shop to do the repairs. We were in our destination town, but at the opposite end from where John Coe and his family were waiting. After the car was repaired, we continued across town where we found the Coe family still waiting to welcome us in their warm house filled with odors of delicious food. We were welcomed and led to the kitchen where the supper table was waiting. Our hostess, Dad's aunt, greeted me as I walked into the room.

"Little Junior. We haven't seen you in a coon's age. Come hug mah' neck."

It was 9:30 when we sat down, hungry and happy, at the food-laden table. I think it may have been the latest either family had ever eaten supper. I fell asleep at the table and had to be carried to bed.

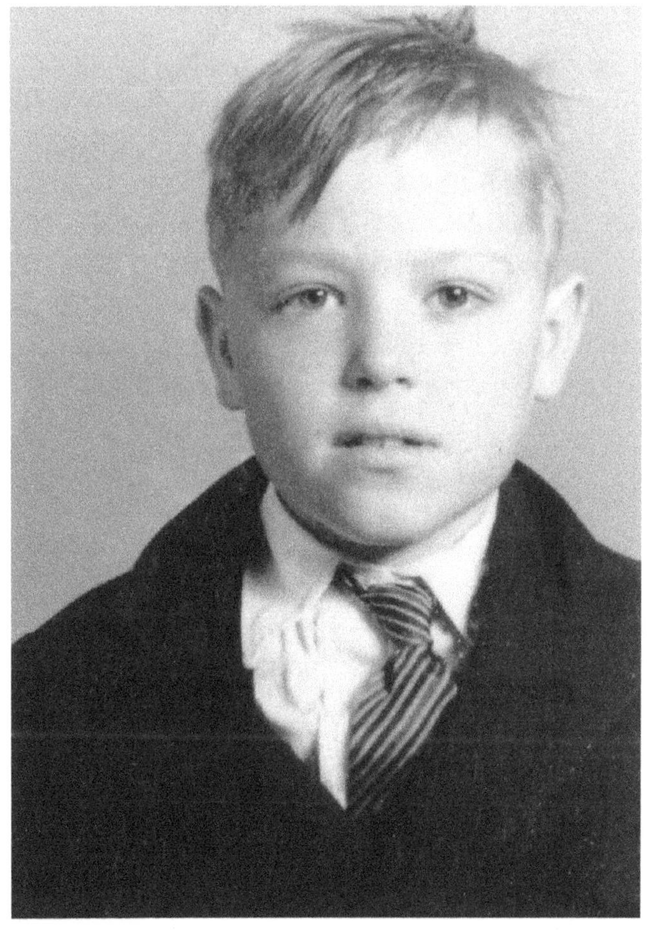

"Little Junior"

KING ARTHUR OF THE SORGHUM PATCH

The Latter-Day Knights

The sorghum harvest was the first farmwork for me as a young boy only five years of age, and it seemed more like play. The sorghum canes were mature, and the seed-heads full and heavy. The canes were ready for harvesting and had to be milled before the first frost. Dad had crafted several long oak blades to be used for stripping the flat, corn-like leaves from the standing canes. The canes were then to be cut with hook-shaped drawknives on long sticks, topped of their seed-heads, and loaded on the wagon for transport to the molasses mill.

Dad handed my playmate Junior and me each one of the medieval-looking oak blades shaped like swords. The handle portion was left rectangular, and the blades shaved to sharp double edges with slightly rounded points. He made us promise no sword fights between us, then demonstrated how to strip the leaves, telling us to always take separate rows and work back-to-back, so as not to accidentally cut each other. After Dad left, we quite suddenly became knights of King Arthur's Round Table, arguing about which of us was Sir Lancelot. After deciding we were Knight Junior and Knight Carroll Junior, and would address each other as "Sir," we set to the task of vanquishing the standing army of the enemy. With much posturing, threatening, grunting, and shouting, we stripped the canes top to bottom, row after row for quite some time—but it was a large field.

We stopped to rest on a grassy tuffet at the end of our rows.

Claiming the leadership role, I told my fellow knight: "Sir Junior, I'll guard our camp while you sleep, then we'll trade duties." Soon into my watch, Dad appeared carrying his own sword.

"What are you boys doing?" he asked.

"We're knights at rest before the next battle," I told him.

Dad declared himself to be King Arthur and joined us for the continued battle. After rousing his knights to action, he took two rows at once, while we took singles. When we finished off the sorghum army, Dad declared us both brave knights, and with a smile, said:

"It's a very good thing the sorghum army couldn't fight back." He then quickly added, "Because there were so many of them."

I was in school and not around for the cutting, topping, and loading of the canes, but Dad took me with him on the cane-loaded wagon to the sorghum mill the next day, which was a Saturday.

"You'll get to see how the sorghum mill works, and you can play in the pummy pile," he said.

"What's that?" I asked.

"Pummies are the flattened canes after the juice has been squeezed out," he explained.

The mill was located on a creek several miles from our farm. The pressing mill itself was uphill from the big, oak-fired, copper pan, called the cooker, where the sweet cane juice was cooked to become molasses. The pan was near the creek, the source of water for its complete washing down at the end of each batch.

The mill press had top and bottom rollers and was powered by a mule walking in a circle around it pulling an overhead beam that turned the rollers. A worker fed canes into the press, and the squeezed juice flowed through a pipe to a vat further down the hill and fed into the cooker pan as needed. The pummies were carted over to the wagon as each armload of new cane was brought to the press.

A father and two sons who lived nearby operated the mill and were paid with a portion of the molasses yield. One son fed the oak wood fire to keep an even temperature, and his father worked the juice from one compartment to another as it thickened, until it was finished molasses at the downhill end of the pan. As Dad's help was part of the deal, he carried canes and pummies. This was a job he didn't like, as he was anxious to work with the cook. He knew the attentiveness and skill of the cook could make a difference between bad, good, or great molasses, so he insisted on switching jobs with a son so he could watch and encourage the cook during the finishing process.

I roamed the mill site exploring everything but stayed away from the hot cooker. As it cooked, the juice formed a green scum at the surface, which the worker skimmed off and threw into a deep pit next to the pan. I was also told to stay away from the skimming pit, and not to get in the path of the mule. Later, Dad told me,

"Get out of the way and go play on the pummy pile until we're finished."

Dad traded-off with the brother who worked with the father at the cooker as the syrup was finishing off. He also helped pour the finished molasses into gallon buckets and sealed them with tin lids to take home. We left the mill with a wagonload of pummies that, along with the sorghum seed tops already in the barn, would be used for silage, or feed, for the animals. At the front of the wagon, we had more than enough buckets of sorghum to last the family for a year, and Dad was verbally calculating, at fifty cents a gallon, how much money he would get at market for the extra molasses.

When we arrived home, Mother was first pleased with the sorghum yield and then upset at how sticky I was, hair to feet, from playing in the pummy pile. After being stripped and washed down, I prepared for supper, where I knew our new molasses would be tasted. At the tasting, Dad, after some deliberation, declared it to be "good, brimming on the verge of great." Our family wanted each crop to be better than the last. We were not disappointed. After a month or so of allowing the molasses to "settle," it would again be taste-tested and compared to last year's crop. Nobody said so, but I think we all expected a "great" designation at the next tasting.

I thought our sorghum cane battle had been well fought. Dad was the sorghum master and our King Arthur of the sorghum patch. As we sat at our tasting, I lamented that our dining table wasn't round.

THE MASTER TRAPPER

My friend Junior and I were getting better with our slingshots. After practicing with cans on a fence and an occasional blue-bellied lizard kill, we still couldn't get close enough to birds and rabbits to get a good shot.

"We're tolerable good at shootin' but we can't get anythin' big enough to eat," Junior lamented.

We wanted to get something we could bring to the table for food. We might have put our efforts into fishing but there was no river or creek nearby with sizable fish. Our local streams produced only crawdads, which were tasty little creatures, but our yield was never enough for anything like a meal. Our fathers wouldn't allow us to have guns for hunting, so our thoughts and curiosity turned to trapping, something neither of us knew much about.

We had both tried what we called "box traps," where a basket or other container is propped up with a stick tied to a long string leading to the hidden trapper. After spreading bait, usually breadcrumbs, in a trail leading to more bait under the basket, the trapper waits for the birds, squirrels, or whatever creatures to be lured in. A yank of the string trips the trigger, and the basket falls over the prey.

Neither of us had caught anything with such devices. I had once thought I would freeze to death lying in the snow with a trigger string in my mittened hand waiting for snowbirds to take the bait, only to lose them when I lifted the trap. Junior and I agreed we needed a better system.

After some discussion, Junior allowed as how he had a kinsman, a Mr. Scarlett, who knew "everythin' about trappin'." He had trapped for pelts in his earlier years, and Junior claimed that he was, in fact, a Master Trapper. Junior soon arranged for us to meet with him for a consultation one day after school out in front of Junior's family barn.

When we arrived, Mr. Scarlett was standing near a wooden bench next to the barn, looking absent-mindedly off into the horizon, but in such a strange way that I had the feeling he was seeing well beyond it. He was a square, heavy-set fellow with gray hair and beard, dressed in farmer's blue-denim bib overalls and a blue shirt. The sun-darkened skin of his face looked stiff as whitleather and emphasized the brightness of his pale blue eyes. Junior, usually a good talker, introduced us but then fell silent, leaving the consultation to me.

Mr. Scarlett sat himself down heavily onto the bench, leaving us standing in front of him. He slowly shifted his weight onto one buttock, released a long, high-pitched fart that ended in a question mark and, pleased with himself, smiled and said:

"Now then. You boys want to learn how to trap small animals."

Junior didn't respond. I said:

"Yes, sir. Our daddies won't give us guns yet—we're too young. We want to trap some rabbit and squirrel, and maybe a big bird or two."

"Have you heard you can catch grouse by sprinklin' salt on their tails?" Scarlett asked with a smile.

"Yes, sir. I've done heard that one," I said, returning his smile.

I sensed that Scarlett was skeptical of our ability to follow through on anything he might tell us, but he got right to business.

"Well," he said, "trappin' is a complicated thing, you see. You have to know a lot about the animal you're workin' with before you can even start. If it's a bait-set trap, you have to know what it eats, and if the bait has to be live or dead. If it's a trail-set trap, you have to know where he travels every day, or days, and what time he walks the trail."

Scarlett described homemade traps as being of two kinds—deadfalls and snares—saying that either can be made by a trapper using only a good pocket knife, a hand ax, and some stout cord.

"I like the deadfall best," he said. "For a deadfall, you build a bait pen by drivin' saplin' stakes well into the ground in a square or circle pattern and cover it with saplin' logs weighted down with rocks. To reach the bait, the animal has to enter the pen at a small openin' where you set the trigger. When it's triggered, a suspended weight—a log or rock—falls on the animal killin' it instantly."

Ending his last sentence, he brought his right hand down onto his left with a loud clap. He ticked off the advantages of the deadfall:

"It's the most humane way to kill the animal; they die instantly with no warnin' to others; doesn't damage the pelt; no cost; no weight to carry along the trapper's trail; and they can be reused. The deadfall is so quick," he continued, "I've killed skunk without their ever leavin' a scent."

This was getting complicated. Pelts are fine, but I wondered if we could eat an animal that had been squashed by a rock. There must surely be a simple trap or snare for a squirrel or rabbit. The snares Scarlett described sounded even harder to do. His favorite example was a spring-pole snare—a noose made of wire or stout cord.

"You scout out the animal's trail, find and strip a saplin' beside its path, bend it down, and connect it to the snare with a baited trigger device. When triggered, the saplin' snaps back up holdin' the noosed animal, which hangs there till the trapper comes back to take it."

I couldn't imagine snaring a squirrel and having him hang there crying a day or so before I skinned him to eat. It was pretty clear we wouldn't be able to do any of the trapping Scarlett described, especially his trigger mechanisms. From his descriptions, the triggers were hand-carved devices that might have required skill and years of practice. Junior seemed to be on the same thought path when he finally found his voice.

"Did you ever use these traps and snares to catch squirrels or rabbits?" Junior asked.

"No," Scarlett said. "I shoot squirrels and rabbits. I used the traps to get marten, mink, ermine, fox, coon, and a couple of beavers oncest."

I had heard of but never seen most of the animals he described. Except for coon and fox, I was sure they didn't live here anymore.

"I used to shoot turkey too," he said, "but we don't have them here no more."

I thought the steel traps, like the ones I'd once seen hanging in my uncle's barn might be the best thing for squirrel and rabbit, so I asked Scarlett about them. As I asked the question, a darkness came across his face. After hesitating a bit, he said,

"You boys don't want to do that. Steel traps are bad. You might catch your own dog, or somebody else's dog, or your brother, or cousin." Scarlett told us how he had seen where animals caught in steel traps had gnawed a leg off below the trap jaws to escape. He mentioned too, that some trappers set steel traps under water to catch beaver, which killed the beaver by drowning. "Just imagine a water animal like a beaver dyin' that way," he said.

I thought it awful too—animals gnawing their leg off to get free and beavers being drowned. The Master Trapper continued his disdain for steel traps by describing how trap makers devised a webbed jaw trap that would prevent the animal from gnawing its leg off to get free.

"I don't trap any longer," Scarlett said, trying to bring some brightness back to the conversation.

"I just hunt sometimes," he added.

"Why did you stop trappin'?" Junior asked.

"Two reasons, I guess. The animals have been drove out by clearing for farmland, and the ones left over have been trapped-out with steel traps."

This seemed to be the end of his answer, but Junior persisted. "What was the other reason, sir?"

"Hard to explain," he said. "When you get to know the animals like I did, they get to be close and personal. Some of them that took a while to catch got to know me too. We were enemies, workin' for our own survival, and both knew it."

Struggling to his feet, he said: "I have to leave you boys now. I've got pigs to feed. I'd advise you both to wait a while till you can shoot a rifle or shotgun, and in the meanwhile, get your daddies to take you huntin' with them. You boys won't be needin' any traps."

After saying his goodbye, his eyes left us and resumed their far-off look of one who has always lived wild and apart. Our Master Trapper turned and headed for his horizon.

RURAL ELECTRIFICATION

A Shocking Story

After we had lived in the Bettis place for several years, Mr. Bettis appeared at our door with news that an electrical power line was to be installed along the main road near our house, and that power would be extended to the farmhouse where we lived. This was great news to all of us, including Mr. Bettis himself, who clearly brimmed with joy. It was especially good news for our family, as we never dreamed that electrical service would ever be connected to rural farms like ours. The opportunities seemed enormous. Dad told us the Rural Electrification Agency, or REA as it was called, had been formed by the government in 1935 or 1936.

"I knew electricity was supposed to come," he said, "but didn't expect anything to happen for another twenty years or so and didn't think it would extend this far out from town. But here it is, 1940, and it's at our door."

To Mr. Bettis, a prideful person to begin with, this singular opportunity meant his farm he lived on and the one leased to our family had both suddenly become seriously more valuable. For us, this was an opportunity to change our lives for the better. Our world was one of kerosene lamps and lanterns, and hand-operated equipment and appliances. We were too far from any ice house to keep an ice box, and what food was not canned, preserved, or dried was kept cool in the spring house—mostly milk, butter, and cheese. In winter we made ice cream, which we called "snow cream," using fresh snow. Once or twice in the summer, for a special picnic, we hauled a block of ice out from Quitman, the closest town. We chipped it up for iced tea and for use, along with rock salt, in our hand-cranked ice cream maker. With electricity, we might even be able to buy a Frigidaire to save food from spoilage and to make ice and even ice cream. We hauled our domestic water up in buckets from the spring down the hill from our house. It wasn't far, but the hill was steep. We had joyful thoughts of water pumps, flush toilets, and maybe even a washing machine. These thoughts were damped, however, by the question in the back of everyone's mind as to whether we could afford these things.

A few months later, the REA workmen installed creosote-coated power poles along our quarter-mile farm road to carry the service line up from the main line, or "high line," along the county road. The last pole for the service line was to be across the farm road from our house. This pole location was on a rock-covered flat area requiring dynamite blasting, which the REA team called a "fire-hole pole."

The two-man fire-hole team, Buddy and Curley, soon arrived and started chipping at the rock to hand-carve a hole for the dynamite. Curley, the bald one of the two and also the fat one, sat holding a star-drill spike on the surface of the rock while skinny Buddy swung a large sledge hammer within inches of Curley's head, repeatedly striking the drill, which Curley rotated after each blow. It made my heart jump to see how close he was coming to Curley's skull, and Dad commented on how dangerous it was. Curley said he trusted Buddy's ability and had for a long time. They dismissed our concern and continued, as Dad and I left the scene of what we considered an accident just waiting to happen.

With the hole prepared, the team, having survived the sledge hammer and drill work, placed the explosives and fuse in the newly formed hole. Before detonation, they asked our entire family to occupy the room in our house furthest from the fire hole. Dad had them wait until he'd moved the green Dodge into the barn just to be sure it wasn't damaged. What an excitement it was. After hearing someone shout "fire in the hole!" there was a huge earthshaking blast, followed by rock chips of all sizes raining down around the blast site with some falling on our roof and around the house. The blast was repeated a second time to produce a hole deep enough to receive the pole.

The REA team soon installed the pole, and in a few days, the overhead wires were strung and connected to a switch box they had attached to our house. An REA electrician consulted Mother as to location of light fixtures, wall switches, and wall outlets for plug-in cords. Grandma was skeptical and fretful about the "electrification" of the house, thinking it was unsafe. She had her own notion as to how electricity must be dealt with. To her, it was an invisible energy, or spirit, which flowed through the wires to the light sockets and wall plugs and would leak out if a light bulb was missing from its base. She fretted also about leakage from the two-slot wall outlets, saying: "This leaking electricity will be dangerous for us. It'll ruin our health."

On the day the electricians were wiring the house, Dad accommodated her concern by installing bulbs in the light sockets to be used for lighting, and screwing fuse plugs into any empty sockets where light wasn't needed and where electricity might leak out. He convinced her, somehow, that the openings in the two-slot wall outlets were too small to allow much, if any, electricity to escape, and she seemed satisfied with his solution.

With electrical power now installed, our house was a new and different environment. We had bright lights we could easily read by, no kerosene odor, and the fascinating ability to plug appliances into the wall outlets. Our first appliance purchase was an electric iron for Mother. She had always complained about building a fire, especially in summer, to heat her flatirons for pressing clothes.

"Now," Dad told her as he presented the new purchase, "you can heat the iron without heating the house."

Mother was pleased, and so was I, as I was allowed to be the first person to plug the iron cord into the wall outlet.

One day soon after, I was lolling about after school, lying on stacked sacks of grain stored in an alcove off the open, dog-trot corridor that separated the two wings of our house. The alcove was meant for storing firewood, but Dad used it in the summer to store feed for livestock. A thick, paper identification tag was wired to the top corner of each sack, and I enjoyed removing the wires and bending them into shapes resembling people and animals. While doing this, I noticed the electrician had installed an electrical outlet in the alcove. With wire in hand, I playfully said "I'm going to plug-IN-N-N-N-N!" as I fell off the sacks in reaction to the shock and bright flash. I was surprised at my stupidity, and when I recovered from the electric shock, declared myself a damn fool, swearing never to tell anyone. After that experience, I was more respectful of electricity and decided that Grandma just might be right, and the energy, or spirit, could leak out if the source wasn't plugged. I learned it took only a small wire to let the spirit out.

Years later as an adult and an architect, I thought of our farmhouse electrification each time I drew symbols for wall outlets on floor plans, labeling each as "co" for "convenience outlet." One day I described Grandma's theory of electricity to an electrician on one of my construction sites. He said that hers was as good an explanation of electricity as any other he had heard. But, unlike my grandma, he didn't seem at all worried about the "leakage." He seemed more concerned about touching a hot wire. I shared that concern with him.

THE FIFTH SUNDAY

Late one Friday afternoon, I'd just returned from wandering the fields with a friend and his dogs, and came into the house through the back porch. I opened the kitchen door and walked into the warm and wonderful odor of butterbeans and ham hocks, reminding me I had helped gather the fresh beans that morning. Mother gave me a glass of iced tea, poured one for herself, and we went to the living room to cool down.

"Your dad will be here soon," she said, and I saw she had brought a tea for him too. Dad walked in carrying three songbooks in his hand and said: "The Fifth Sunday's coming up in two days. Are we all ready?" Only six years old, I didn't yet know about the Fifth Sunday, or what it was, but Mother, of course, did.

"I have the picnic dinner all planned," she said. "Have you practiced your new songs?"

"I'll be doing that now," Dad replied. "Come sing with me when you can."

It was a very warm afternoon, and Dad went out to the front porch. We soon heard his tenor voice drifting through the screen door. He tried and re-tried singing the new songs and wanted to learn two from each book. After the corn bread was in the oven, Mother went out to join him, adding her alto voice to the effort. That evening Mother and Dad explained that the Fifth Sunday was a "Singing Sunday." We would be going to another township for the singing and would be there all day. There seemed little for me to be excited about, but I always enjoyed seeing other places outside our local area and began looking forward to the outing.

Our family always sang songs for fun, and our parents taught us many songs and sayings as part of everyday life. We whistled too, but Dad did most of it. He whistled while doing his chores around the farm and had a technique that included whistling in as well as whistling out, giving different sounds. With some tunes, the result sounded like two whistlers rather than one. What he loved best however, was singing, and the church choir just wasn't enough for him. "Too much preachin' and not enough singin'," he declared. He joined a serious singing group and was assigned tenor in their quartet. The group practiced often, bought new song books as they were published, and often practiced the new songs together. Their music was what we call gospel music, printed with shaped notes and bound in 5" x 8" songbooks with titles like *Gospel Treasures*, *Grateful Praise*, or *Roses of Spring*. The songbooks were published by the Stamps-Baxter Music Co. of Dallas, Texas, or the Hartford Music Publishing Co. of Hartford, Arkansas.

The general "singings" were not like group singing in church services or church choirs, but separate and different. Although this system of music used gospel themes, and the singings were often held in churches, they were organized outside the church and not done for worship. Participants just wanted the joy of singing, and the gospel music system was available for their use. This fit well for our family as we weren't faithful churchgoers.

In addition to singing events occasionally arranged for the groups and their audiences after church services on Sundays, the big event for the gospel singers was the Fifth Sunday Singing, scheduled in advance for each month that had a fifth Sunday. Depending on schedules, some Singing Sundays weren't on the fifth. In all these events, singers joined other similar groups for an entire day of music, and those occurring in the summer were referred to as an "all-day singing with dinner-on-the-ground," as they had a potluck picnic dinner midday. The food was usually spread out under a shade tree on tablecloths and blankets on the ground, or on temporary, make-shift tables made of boards supported by saw-horses.

I attended many singings over the years, but the one I remember most was the first Fifth Sunday event we attended that weekend. Our family arrived mid-morning, along with all the other singers, at a country church in an adjacent township. It took some effort to get there, and some folks came from quite a distance away. Dad mentioned that a soprano, Bonny Wright, from a quartet he had sung with before, would be at the event, and singing organizers Fred Cromwell and Loy Foust were also to attend.

I didn't recognize many of the people there, but Dad seemed to know almost everyone, greeting them with handshakes and smiles, introducing some of them to Mother.

At the appointed time, people filed into the church house and seated themselves on the long benches. It was a hot day, and the tall windows were open for ventilation. The women, in their summer flowered-print dresses, fanned themselves using cardboard fans with wooden handles, some with floral patterns but most with an advertisement for the Olmstead Funeral Home in nearby Heber Springs. The men had, of course, removed their Sunday straw hats when entering the church, and were using them as fans. The only young folks around were several girls I didn't know, and Bart Badders, a boy my age who lived a few miles from us. Bart and I talked, and decided we'd try to skip the singing and play instead.

When most everyone was inside the church, some seated and some standing, the church pastor stood at the pulpit and greeted everyone. With a smile, he announced his great pleasure at hosting the "all-day dinner with singing-on-the-ground." After waiting for the laughter, he introduced the singing director, Fred Cromwell, who was to lead the program. As the director started helping the singers arrange themselves by singing parts, Dad joined the tenors, Sis the sopranos, and Mom led little Alder Lee and me to the alto section. I asked her if I could stay outside and play with Bart Badders, and she agreed, knowing my restlessness. She handed me one of our portable telescoping aluminum drinking cups. The metal cup held water when opened and after use, collapsed into itself and the mouth covered with a slip-on decorative cap for easy portability.

"Use that drinking cup," she said. "I don't want you to get mud on your knees drinking from a branch."

I was pleased to have this ingenious device and put it into my pocket.

"You can go play with the Badders boy, but don't get too dirty, don't wander too far off, and watch out for snakes, you hear?"

"Yes, ma'am."

Outside I found Bart leaning against a car.

"So, you got out too?" I asked.

Yep," he said. "Didn't wanna get stuck inside for hours. It's gonna be noisy in there."

As the choir began with their scales, Bart and I climbed a narrow pathway up a steep hill behind the church house during their warm-up: "Do Re Mi Fa So La Ti Do. Do Ti La So Fa Mi Re Dooo."

We began repeatedly running down the hill, testing our skill at barely keeping our legs moving fast enough under our gravity-accelerated bodies. As a first song, the choir launched into a lively all-parts chorus of the joyful "I'll Fly Away." With the tall casements full open to the cooling air and to song, we were getting a loud rendition of the singers' "flight." We both knew the song from church services and on each run down the hill, inspired by the song, we held out our arms, waving them in pretended flight.

"I-I-I-I'll fly away (oh glory!). I-I-I-I'll fly away (in the morning). When I die hallelujah by and by- I-I-I-I'll fly away!"

After chatting with Bart and comparing pocket knives, I saw from the top of the hill, another, narrower pathway down. I launched myself downhill as I had before on the other path but realized part-way down that it led into a three-strand barbed wire fence. Unable to stop, I gave a short leap, so the top wire hit me in the chest instead of the throat. I felt the barbs bite into my chest and legs and knew my clean white shirt and probably my pants were ruined with rips and blood. *This is worse than mud on my knees*, I thought. As the choir started a new song at that same moment, I heard their voices swell, then taper their volume as a soprano began an aria-like solo. It was the most beautiful music I had ever heard, and difficult to describe. She had a clear, bell-like voice, similar, as I later learned, to that of Joan Baez. Captivated by her voice, I stayed there bleeding, partly leaning, partly hanging on the wire fence, and listened until she had finished her solo.

Bart had caught up with me and was looking on.

"Boy-howdy!" he said. "You've sure done it to yourself this time."

He helped me unhook the barbs without doing worse damage to either my body or clothing and used his handkerchief to wipe up blood and press the barb punctures to stop the bleeding. We found a nearby branch, drank some water from the folding cup and mopped up some more blood. I went back into the church leaving Bart outside to wander on his own. I wanted to hear the soloist again and watch her sing. Finding a spare chair behind the back bench, I sat listening to every song. I could occasionally hear Dad's voice among the tenors, but the fine, perfect, angelic voice I wanted most to hear did not solo again nor could I hear it in the soprano section.

When the singers broke for the picnic dinner, I joined my parents and asked Dad who the soprano soloist was. Before he could answer, Mother noticed the sad condition of my clothing, saw the blood, and began a detailed inspection of my wounds.

"What in the dickens have you done to yourself?" she demanded. "This is worse than mud on your knees. Are you badly hurt? Let me look at you."

I knew no food would be served or eaten by this family until my reprimand had been delivered. She examined my wounds, did some dabbing with her own handkerchief, and delivered an admonition for the remains of the day:

"No more of this rough stuff. After dinner, you're not to go out in the woods. You either stay right here in the churchyard or sit in the church house with us."

As the "dinner-on-the-ground" was ending and food baskets being re-packed, Dad walked me over to where Cromwell stood engaged in a lively discussion with a thin, attractive, young woman and introduced them to me.

"This is your soloist, son. This is Bonny Wright, and this gentleman is Mr. Cromwell. Fred, Bonny, this is my boy, Carroll Junior."

I'd heard the name before and knew Mother didn't much like her. Probably, I later thought, because she was an attractive, single woman, friendly with Dad and spending time with him in the same quartet.

I stood transfixed in front of Miss Wright, looking up at her, not able to utter a single word. Dad helped by saying: "Carroll here likes your singing. He's a fan of yours."

Miss Wright smiled and thanked me. Speechless, I continued looking up at her, and Dad had to remind me to shake hands with Mr. Cromwell.

Outside the church, I told Bart I would be in the church house singing with my folks and wouldn't be playing with him in the afternoon. I went to the tenor section with Dad, who shared his songbooks with me. The first piece sung in the afternoon included another wonderful solo by Bonny Wright. I could have listened to that voice forever. She made me want to sing. This was the beginning of my appreciation of music, which has followed me ever since. I'll sing forever, I told myself that day.

No. 179
I'll Fly Away
Copyright, 1932, in "Wonderful Message"
Hartford Music Co., owner
A. E. B.
Albert E. Brumley
1. Some glad morn-ing when this life is o'er, I'll fly a-
2. When the shad-ows of this life have grown,
3. Just a few more wea-ry days and then, fly a-way
way; To a home on God's ce-les-tial shore,
fly a-way; To a land where joys shall nev-er end,
Like a bird from pris-on bars has flown,
Refrain
I'll fly a-way. I'll fly a-
fly a-way, fly a-way. fly a-way,
way, O glo-ry, I'll fly a-way; When I die,
fly a-way, in the morning,
Hal-le-lu-jah, by and by, I'll fly a-way.
fly a-way, fly a-way.

TRADE DAY IN QUITMAN

Trade day was coming up in our local town of Quitman, the closest town to the Bettis Place, and I was excited to be going along. Sis would be staying home and minding our little brother, Alder Lee, and I would ride to the event with Mother and Dad in the green Dodge. As we took to the road, I had the back seat to myself and watched the landscape passing by, waiting in anticipation of the Burma Shave road signs I knew would appear around halfway to our destination. We were all fans of the signs, and we each had selected our favorite one. I liked all of them I could understand, and had memorized only one:

> *Past school houses;*
> *Take it slow;*
> *Let our little;*
> *Shavers grow:*
> *Burma Shave.*

We discussed each of our favorites. Sis's favorite we knew was:

> *The answer to;*
> *A maiden's prayer;*
> *Is not a chin;*
> *Of stubby hair:*
> *Burma Shave.*

Mother's favorite was:

His tenor voice;
She thought divine;
Till whiskers scratched;
Sweet Adeline:
Burma Shave.

Dad's favorite I couldn't understand at first, but he explained it and helped me memorize it:

I proposed to Ida;
Ida refused;
Ida won my Ida;
If Ida used:
Burma Shave.

We were still laughing when the signs appeared, all hoping there would be a new one we hadn't already seen. They assigned me to read them off, and as they appeared I read:

Maybe you can't;
Shoulder a gun;
But you can shoulder;
The cost of one;
Buy Defense Bonds.

We were silenced for a moment or two, coming down from the rollicking joy the signs had always given us. "The war has ruined everything," Dad said, "even the Burma Shave signs."

I was happy to be visiting Quitman again. As we entered town, there was the grist mill on the left where we took our corn for grinding into cornmeal, and then the cotton gin Dad had taken me to once with a load of cotton, then came our downtown destinations.

Arriving in town, Mother and Dad separated to complete their shopping, and my role was to "help" Dad with his purchases. Mother's list always included dress patterns, fabric, and thread. She always hoped to find the newest, most fashionable patterns that followed the images in the magazines. She couldn't always find patterns in her petite size but would select the next closest size available and make the necessary adjustments. As a skilled seamstress, she could work wonders with her treadle-operated Singer sewing machine. She always had a few household supplies on her list, such as castor oil, Mercurochrome, gauze, and surgical tape for our many scuffs, cuts, and bruises. She also bought some powdered chocolate for making desserts and some rock candy to reward my sister and brother for enduring our absence.

I went with Dad to the harness shop to pick up a new bridle he'd ordered.

"Which fool mule of yours is getting the bridle?" asked the harnesser.

"The only fool I have. The youngest, feistiness one— Andy," Dad replied. "He's hard to manage and this bigger bit is for better control of him."

With the new bridle over his shoulder and the empty kerosene can in his hand, Dad led me to the general store. As we walked in, a "Howdy, Carroll" greeting came from several directions. The clerk and several shoppers knew Dad, so handshakes and greetings went round. The clerk re-filled the kerosene can and discussed livestock medications with Dad, settling on a large bottle of horse liniment for our purchase. Dad stocked up on his smoking tobacco, always selecting the Prince Albert brand. I loved the tin box it came in, shaped flat to fit into a pocket. The tin was a beautiful color of red with a full-length image of the prince, in a long coat and with a cane, on its sides. The clerk teased Dad by suggesting another popular brand, Bull Durham, which was packaged in a cloth drawstring bag with a round paper tab on the strings.

"We both know that's bad tobacco," Dad said. "'Bull Manure' would be a better name for it." Along with his purchases, Dad bought us each a co-cola. Much of the time on trade day was spent socializing and exchanging news with friends, neighbors, and acquaintances. Dad and I joined a group of men there for the day, gathered outside the general store. They were discussing crops, the war, prices, and their health in their soft, slow voices. Almost all were wearing a fresh, white, newly ironed shirt with chino-beige trousers, while a few wore their denim-bib work overalls. They greeted each other, always asking how they were. The answers often came in terms of cotton grades used when selling cotton, "fair to middlin'" being one of their favorites.

I was becoming bored and took hold of Dad's chino pocket and asked: "Dad, can I have a nickel to buy some candy?"

I looked up to see it wasn't Dad. The man smiled down saying: "I'll just refer you to your real dad, young sir."

I got my nickel but was embarrassed and wished I was tall enough to see faces better. As we stood there, someone noticed an elderly man walking along the other side of the street and commented,

"There goes old man Jenkins. I thought he was long dead."

Another said: "Nope. He's still much alive. I expect he might even stamp the dirt in on all of us."

Laughter and joking was always a part of the conversations. Much of the discussion, however, was about the war. I later thought that absent the war, each of the men might have assigned a higher cotton grade to his health and welfare.

As the crowd of visitors started thinning out, we loaded the Dodge with our purchases. Sharing the back seat with our supplies, I arranged to sit on the right side so I could easily read the Burma Shave signs again on the way back. But I somehow knew the joyfulness of the signs that we had felt before was now gone.

The Orange Box

It was 1941, and I was age seven. In the first year of WWII, the world was changing in far-off places. Life on our farm, however, continued its usual struggle with little change, except for rationing and more scarcity. But the arrival of an orange box changed our lives in unexpected ways.

One day I was with Mother as she was placing some papers in the family trunk where we stored documents and keepsakes. Along one end of the trunk, I saw a stack of four-by-eight, stiff paper rectangles with holes punched in them and bound into bundles with twine. I asked what they were.

"Vouchers," she said. "These are cancelled checks that prove we've paid a bill or satisfied a debt." Holding one up, she said: "Read the word made by the punched holes."

I read aloud: "P-A-I-D." Amazed there were so many, I asked how we got the money to pay them all.

"We don't always have enough money to pay all the bills on time, and sometimes we pay late," she said. After a gentle, almost imperceptible sigh, she added, "But we always get them paid."

I didn't know then, of course, but a few years later I learned how farm families like ours borrowed money from the bank each year for seed, fertilizer, equipment, and animal feed. As we harvested and sold the crops later in the year, the loans would be repaid, with interest, and the money left over after paying the bank, the mortgage or lease, and other expenses, was the earnings. These earnings were becoming less and less each year as farm prices for what we grew declined. Rolling the debt over to the next year was a recipe for disaster, possibly leading to the cancellation of a lease or loss of the farm to a loan foreclosure.

Life on our farm, as with all the other family farms, meant producing cash crops for our outside income, growing as much of our own food as we could, and selling any excess when possible. This was hard work for the entire family. Everyone had his or her role to play and their assigned duties to perform. Dad was our mainstay. His job was especially difficult and hazardous, and any misstep, accident, illness, or injury could jeopardize the edgy balance of having enough food to eat and cash income to pay the bills. Dad had already suffered a nasty bout of malaria and an injury from a stump puller in a land-clearing accident. I'm sure the prospect of losing his good health was of some concern to our parents and grandparents, who had to pay close attention to such things. With diseases and potential injuries, our livelihood traced a thin line between success and failure.

To achieve the financial survivor's advantage, many of the farmers used their skills at hunting and fishing. Other skills included hand-fabricating craft products—produced in the wintertime when crops demanded less or little work—and selling the crafts to supplement their farm income. Dad came from a family of tobacco farmers who were also craftsmen. In addition to farm income, they earned cash by selling their craft products under a large tree beside the county road. They sold carved butter molds, churn plungers, baskets, whirligigs, woven baskets, and plug chewing tobacco.

At the Bettis Place, Dad continued with his skill as a basket maker, working out of the stone-walled storage space that formed the lower story under our kitchen. He split green, white-oak wood with an ax and frow, and shaped the pliable wood with a drawing knife to provide the withes for weaving. He sold these tough and durable baskets to other farmers for handling their harvests. The sizes he sold were half, full, and double bushel. He hauled them to Quitman, the closest town, where they were sold at the general store.

Dad was also skilled at cutting hair with hand-clippers. When electrical service was extended to our house, he bought a set of electric clippers and began giving haircuts to the men in our township, charging them a fair price for the service. He gave cuts free, now and again, to those he knew could not afford it, or whose sartorial shagginess offended him. He was also good at carpentry and could occasionally get a job helping build a house or barn, but more often he worked on the construction or repair of a school or church, donating his labor.

To us children, none of the difficulty of making a living was apparent. We had a good family life, always had enough good food to eat, and every day seemed new and interesting. Craftwork was done on the farm or in the township, and Dad never had to leave home for work outside the community.

I began to understand, however, the necessity of Dad's outside, non-farming work on the day our RFD postman delivered a wooden box of an unusual shape, shipped to us from the mail order company of Montgomery Ward. It was about two feet by three feet, but only about five inches deep, and painted a bright orange color. Sis and I were very curious about this orange box that had just entered our life, but Mother was noncommittal as to what it was.

When Dad came in from the field, we all gathered round for the opening. The box had a handle at the top and hinges along its spine. He cut the shipping ties and opened it, revealing a display of carpentry tools attached to both sides of the interior. It contained a hand saw, hammer, brace and bits, a metal framing square, a hand-ax, drawing knife, and a folding, yellow, wood ruler for measuring. Dad then explained to Sis and me something Mother already knew—that he was going to the town of Stuttgart, more than a hundred miles away, to work as a carpenter at the Army airfield being built near there. The work, as we learned later, was construction of buildings to house an Army Air Corps training facility for glider and twin-engine aircraft pilots.

This was a new turn of events. Dad and Mother had lengthy discussions about how the farm would be managed in his absence, but we had no notion as to how long he would be gone.

"I'll stay there as long as the job lasts and come home as often as I can," he said.

Grandma would come to stay with us while he was gone, to help with the chores and taking care of me and three-year-old Alder Lee. Helen Marie at age thirteen was old enough that she could also help.

A week or so later, Dad left the house at dawn with a suitcase in one hand and the orange box in the other, to meet his pre-arranged ride at the county road down the hill from our house.

* * * * *

It was a strange feeling having Dad gone. Helen Marie and I attended school and helped with the chores as best we could. We were visited by Mother's brothers and her father from time to time, and Grandma was always there. But the days seemed sad and empty with Dad gone. He had sold the pigs and the fatted calf he was raising for beef. Our family team fed the remaining animals and milked the cows, but everyone was afraid of the mules. They were fed in their crib with corn and other feed but were left to go from the barn to the pasture at will, and they seemed wilder by the week.

After what seemed like a long time, Dad came home for a visit during a break in the construction job. He had helped build classrooms, offices, and barracks for the pilot training operations at the airfield and became the foreman of a construction crew of carpenters. He was home for a brief visit and was to return to Stuttgart in a week to continue his job there. While home, he created a flurry of activity around the farm. The mules, Amos and Andy, had become quite unruly. They were a perfectly matched pair in terms of size and color, with dark-brown bodies and black fetlocks and face markings but were very different in temperament. Andy had been somewhat wild to begin with and had become especially troublesome in Dad's absence. While Dad was trying to hitch the team to his wagon, Andy kicked at him with both feet barely missing his head. In describing the experience, Dad said he could feel the swift air from Andy's hooves on both sides of his head and, but for a few inches' separation, would have been dead that day. This event caused him to re-think how the farm would be handled in the future when he had to return to his outside work, but his immediate concern was dealing with Andy.

Following some tidying up around the farm, Dad took Andy back to the Mitchell Brothers, riding Amos with Andy in tow. The Mitchells operated their horse- and mule-trading business from a large barn and trading yard on the road southeast of the town of Quitman. They had a good reputation as fair traders and did business with almost everyone in our township. Dad wanted to sell Andy back to the Mitchells, and make do with Amos and old Anthony, a mule he had owned for many years—at least until the next planting season. When Dad arrived back home riding Amos and with money in his pocket, he had trouble telling us his story of what happened at the Mitchells. He kept breaking out in laughter and had to keep starting over.

He had told the elder Mitchell brother that Andy, the mule he'd bought from him as part of the team, hadn't been properly broke, and warned him that he spooked easily and could be dangerous. They discussed it for a while, and standing in the auction yard next to

Andy, had agreed on a price to buy him back. The other brother brought the money out to Dad. As the three of them—along with several lollygaggers always found at the trading yard—stood around Andy, Dad was saying goodbye when the elder Mitchell said:

"This mule is going to be just fine. We know how to take care of Ol' Andy here."

As he spoke the last sentence, he slapped Ol' Andy on the rump, whereupon Andy bolted straight ahead, broke wind, ran out the open gate and down the county road at a fast clip.

The usual blatherskite of the knot of men immediately erupted into riotous laughter. Andy didn't stop, as everyone expected. He continued his wild chase down the road and disappeared into an unfenced meadow and the woods beyond. After recovering from the laughter, Dad again said goodbye and rode out of earshot before having another good laugh. We learned later that the Mitchells didn't find Andy for almost a week. He was a dangerous and troublesome mule, but I was left with the notion that Dad respected him for the way he claimed his freedom.

The mule trade was a success, as was Dad's construction job. At the end of the week, he again left the house at sunrise with his suitcase in one hand and the orange box in the other, heading back to Stuttgart to complete his work there.

1941 - 1945

Part III. The Gresham Place

THE GRESHAM PLACE

After some years at the Bettis Place, we moved to a farm owned by my grandfather, John Anderson Gresham, Jr. The Gresham Place, as we called it, was in the same county and township, some six miles further up the main road from the Bettis Place, near the town of Pearson.

Although I considered the Bettis house to be my first home, I felt no regrets in leaving it, perhaps because I already knew and liked Granddad Gresham's house. I had visited there often enough, and under such welcoming circumstances, it felt like a second home to me. Our visits had been mostly holidays and family events, with Granddad, uncles, aunts, and many cousins, so I felt happy about going there to live. Sis had the same feelings about our new home and, after learning she would be attending the same school with her same friends, was in favor of the move.

I don't know all the circumstances of the relocation, but I believe the farm became vacant when Granddad, a widower with no children left at home, gave up farming in favor of travel and adventure. By then, he was spending part of each year in California with his brother Rob and other relatives, and the other part of the year in his hometown of Pearson. However it came about, the move was a positive thing for our family, providing more acreage to farm as well as a newer house and barn.

The Gresham family has owned land in the Pearson community since Minerva Clayton Gresham moved from Kentucky and settled there in the mid-1800s. Minerva lost her husband, Anderson Boyd Gresham, to cholera when he was just thirty-one. She relocated with her six children from the "sickly" Kentucky town of Hickman to the healthier town of Pearson in the Crossroads Township of Cleburne County (then Van Buren County) to settle and raise her children. She sold her property in Kentucky and purchased a 300-acre parcel of land near the town of Pearson where she built the first Gresham house and began farming operations. My grandfather, John Anderson, Jr., was Minerva's grandson, and his farm property that we moved to was likely part of the original acreage.

After the Minerva Gresham house, my great-grandfather built a new house and outbuildings on the Gresham Road site in 1892, when my grandfather was nine years old. Many years later, my granddad John A. Gresham, Jr. in turn, demolished that house and rebuilt another on the site with Dad as his lead carpenter. That was some ten years before our move, so the house was fairly new when we took up residence. The house had been emptied and cleaned, ready for us to move in. Moving help had been arranged, but we all wanted to see it before the movers would arrive the next day.

I already knew how to get to our Gresham House destination from the old Bettis Place and from the back seat of the Green Dodge, I savored the scenes on each leg of the short trip. We drove the familiar route up Highway 25 past the road on the left that led to the town of Pearson and a bit further, turned right on Gresham Road. After climbing a steep hill, the road continued in a gradual incline along an almost-level ridge with parcels of the farm property on each side. Both parcels sloped down from the road to streams running through a pasture and meadow on the right side of the road and through a wooded area on the left. As we continued up the road, Dad commented on his preference for the gently rolling hills of the place.

"This land will be easy to farm, and sloped enough for good drainage of the fields and meadows. It'll be a relief not to work the steeper hills and rocky ridges of the Bettis Place any longer."

On our left was the two-story cottage built by Grandfather in 1906 to live in while the main house was under construction. I had seen the cottage before but didn't know it was part of the farm. As we drove past it, Mother told us she and Dad had lived there the first two years of their married life in the "Little House," as we called it—something we hadn't known before.

Further up the gradually sloping road was the mailbox that served the house with Rural Free Delivery, and then the main house, sited on a level area to our right. Across the road from the house was the large, level orchard with many fruit trees. Although as a child, Mother had lived in the previous house on the site and had spent considerable time in the present one with Granddad, she spoke as if she were seeing it for the first time.

"It's a tranquil place, at peace with itself and its surroundings."

The entry drive led to the house on the right and the barnyard on the left. The house was set back from the road by a broad lawn and was framed by a large oak on one side and an enormous tulip poplar on the other. Shrubbery around the house included lilacs and small catalpa trees. The style of the house, as I was later to learn, was Craftsman. The ample front porch was covered by a gable roof, supported by three sloped, square columns, and connected to the larger gable part of the main house. The exterior walls were ship-lap wood siding, painted white.

The two front entry doors off the porch were puzzling to us, but Dad, who helped build the house, explained.

"It was built," he said "to accommodate two families, if necessary. The main part of the house is split into two halves from front entries to the kitchen and service porch at the back. If shared, each family would have a living room and one or two bedrooms, sharing the dining room, kitchen, and service porch. The twin living rooms have fieldstone fireplaces, back-to-back in the central wall, sharing the same chimney. We'll be using the whole house and have a living and dining room in one side, and three bedrooms in the other, with a fireplace in both the living room and front bedroom."

We toured the house together, imagining our furniture in each of the rooms.

"It seems different when we expect to live here," Mother said. "It's a perfect place for us."

Just inside the front doors, between the front wall and the two fireplaces, was a small room. It had doors to both the living room and the front bedroom—a sort of entry-closet serving both halves. Its small space now featured a life-size photo portrait of Grandmother Sarah Helen Thompson Gresham on one wall, and a family crest, hand-painted on hardboard, on the other. These hangings were to remain, and we later added a small bookcase for the family Bible, a wordbook, and two large volumes of the *Complete Works of Shakespeare*. The photo portrait was the only image I had of my maternal grandmother, who died in a typhoid epidemic at age thirty-two, long before I was born. I later named this curious, little-used room "The Grandmother and Shakespeare room."

As we walked through the living room and dining room to the kitchen, there was another small room at the back of the house, adjacent to the kitchen, which we called the bathroom. Its name was aspirational only, as it had no plumbing. Granddad, who had laid out the floor plan, expected someday to install plumbing in the two adjacent rooms: kitchen and bathroom. The house was wired with electricity at the same time our Bettis Place was electrified, and Granddad felt sure that plumbing would be the next good thing to come but was just not there yet.

A screened service porch behind the kitchen led to an adjoining small, uncovered porch, and from there, two steps down to the backyard. The small porch provided a platform for the drilled well immediately next to it, allowing us to easily draw water from a rope-and-pulley-operated, tall, thin dip-bucket, pour it into a supply pail, and walk the bucketful directly through the screened porch into the kitchen. This was a favorite timesaver and much less work than carrying water buckets up a steep hill from a distant spring as we did at the Bettis Place. Behind the main structure were the smokehouse, storm cellar, chicken house, and privy. There was room for a kitchen garden between the smokehouse and cellar, and there were two cherry trees in the back yard near the chicken house, one bearing red fruit and the other yellow.

In addition to having a newer, well-built house and barn, what also pleased our parents were the storm cellar and the large orchard across the road on the other parcel. After the move, with the improved safety of our storm cellar, we also had a cool place to store the canned, preserved, and dried fruits and vegetables we expected to produce from the orchard and our usual kitchen garden.

Mother was pleased with the cookstove, which had four burner holes and a water reservoir on the side that provided hot water when the stove was fired. The front porch had a view of the front lawn and the orchard across the road, which Dad said had peaches, pears, and several apple varieties. The front porch also included the welcome feature of a porch swing. Made of green-painted hardwood slats, it was suspended from the ceiling by chains and made a smooth, sweeping arc when swung.

All our new neighbors were people our family knew. The Bittle family lived west of our place. Their parcel faced a different road, but theirs and ours touched diagonally at their corner points. Across the road northeast of us were the Todds, whose property faced Highway 25, and southeast where Gresham Road ended at a crossroad, lived Paul Bivens. Next to him was Tom Badders, who'd shared his house and farm with our family some years before.

Soon after moving in, we met our RFD postman, a cheerful Mr. Rankin. He was a very fat person, who drove a green Plymouth sedan with a roof rack for delivery of large items ordered from mail-order catalogues. In that time and place, a fat person was seldom to be seen, as most people, male and female, were lean and thin. We referred to him as "Fatty Rankin," but never to his face, of course. When seated there was no room between the steering wheel and his stomach, and all his shirts and jackets were worn through where the wheel constantly rubbed against his stomach. Neither Dad nor Mother had met him before, but he remembered Mother as the daughter of Anderson Gresham who had once been postmaster in Pearson where Rankin picked up his mail each day for delivery.

It was a joyful experience moving into a well-equipped house. With furnishings in and ready for use, we all went to the front porch, and with the kids in the swing, Mother and Dad stood gazing at the open, level lawn and the orchard across the road.

"This is a place of abundance," Dad said, "and we're lucky to be here." We were all pleased with the amenities of the new house and its surroundings and felt at home already. We hoped the Gresham Place was our setting for the beginnings of an easier life.

QUITMAN SCHOOL

That first summer at the Gresham Place cooled down to its end, and we turned our sights to school. Over the past year, there had been school consolidations. The Bettis School I had attended, along with other one- and two-room schools, merged with the Quitman Public School, which offered grades one through twelve and free bus transportation. Sis already attended Quitman. Mother and Dad were in favor of the consolidation and pleased I was also going to attend there, as it provided more resources for the students than the Bettis School. Like most other one-room schools, Bettis had provided instruction only from grades one through eight, and the teacher's attention was shared by all grades. Although at Bettis, students could progress as fast as they learned the subjects, the going was slow with so many grade levels taught by the same teacher. At Quitman, students were organized into separate classes by grade level, and I would be in classrooms with those my own age (seven), academic grade (third), and with the full-time attention of the teacher.

* * * * *

Sis and I were to catch the school bus a quarter mile from home at Carthyl Swaffer's store on the corner where Pearson Road joins the Quitman Highway. On the first day of school, we waited as the "Blue Bird," which everyone called our bus, came over the hill and down to our corner stop. As it approached us and stopped, I was fascinated by how it was built, and recognized the Ford Double-A Model truck chassis as the base it was built on from bumper to windshield, including the wire wheels. At the windshield, the hand-crafted, wooden coachwork began and continued to the back with windows on both sides and in the rear. The exterior surface was fabricated using one-inch by four-inch, wooden, tongue-and-groove flooring material. The front passenger door, with its own window, had its rear edge trimmed at an angle such that the closed door fit perfectly where it joined the side of the coach. The truck part of the vehicle was black, but the coachwork was painted a beautiful color of blue.

The Blue Bird was driven by a tall, thin man with a prominent Adam's apple, who never spoke a word to anyone. He would stop the bus, open the door with an iron lever mechanism, and when we were inside and seated, close the door, and drive. Sometimes, we would get very noisy in the back, but he just did his driving job and carried on as if hauling cattle, ignoring the loud games, the teasing, and the singing. We quickly came to know our fellow riders, who were mostly different from our classmates at school. Riding the Blue Bird soon became a familiar and pleasant start to the school day and its relaxing end.

The usual walking route to the bus stop, for us and kids from neighboring families, was a shortcut pathway we devised. It led from our house on Gresham Road through our hay meadow, linking to the Quitman Highway at a point across the road from Swaffer's store. Another, more interesting route used by me, the

Badders boys, and others, led through our cow pasture, along the stream bed through some forest, and through someone's private backyard, ending across the road from the bus stop. The girls never took this route, as it was rough and required navigating through several barbed-wire fences. We always arrived in time to catch the bus.

Quitman School had modern, almost-new buildings on a large campus. Many of my classmates were also new in the school due to the recent school consolidations. I had the new experience and pride of having my own desk in my homeroom. As my name was Carroll, my classmates shortened it to "Karo," which in the local vernacular denoted a scrappy person who makes mischief. I wasn't one who "karoed" but was nonetheless proud of my new name. I took the label from a Karo-brand corn syrup container and proudly glued it to the edge of my desk.

Sis took courses in home economics, as did most girls in those days, and also studied music. Being a bright, outgoing girl, she was asked to work as a part-time helper at the school's business office, usually at their front desk as a greeter-facilitator, and was allowed to practice her music on the school's piano.

Quitman School wasn't strong on organized games, but we did play baseball and basketball. The boys my age mostly played marble games and mumblety-peg. I started carrying marbles in my pockets instead of pebbles and my slingshot, which I had done until then. Most of us kept our marbles in a drawstring bag in one front pocket and our slightly bigger shooter, or taw, in the other. We made a circle in the sand and shot marbles almost daily—and always for keep—in a game we called "four-man keepers" with four players.

Frequently, one of the boys who lived nearby rode his pony to school and tethered it to a post near the classroom wing. We took turns riding it during recess and the noon hour. Another boy sometimes brought his pony too, with a sled behind, and we all got rides around the campus. Once, all the boys who had bicycles, though many of us didn't, rode their bikes to school for an informal show-and-tell. I longed to have a bike myself someday.

The only adult-organized and supervised games were baseball on the playing field and classes in the gymnasium. Starting always with calisthenics, these included basketball and some form of dodgeball, neither of which I was any good at. For the most part, we were on our own for play activities, and did whatever we collectively decided might be fun. The older boys helped organize some of these activities and maintained a semblance of order. That worked until the day a dump truck deposited a small mountain of sand for a construction project on campus. We all stood watching, trying to decide what to do with such a windfall. I organized a "construction crew" and created an entire community, including roads winding up the mountain, housing, cars, churches, and schools, all formed with wood chips, sticks, and stones. As the project neared completion, we were invaded by a band of marauders, who declared war and destroyed the entire community. A fight ensued but didn't last long, as the vandals were mostly older, bigger boys than the builders. At home that night, I described our project and its demise to Dad, sharing my realization there were both builders and destroyers amongst us.

Dad told me we had to expect such things and said: "Just remember to always be the creator and not the destroyer."

* * * * *

One day at school, another student and I went early to the boys' restroom near the end of afternoon recess. A minor argument broke out between us as we stood washing our hands at two of the several washbasins along the wall across from the entry door. We began playfully squirting water at each other, directing our dueling streams by holding a hand under the faucet and turning the tap with the other. As another boy appeared at the door, I directed the water at him, and found that, at full flow, the stream would reach the entry door very nicely. The boy had the choice of getting drenched or ducking back out the doorway and leaving. He left. This was fun, so I told my companion, Keith, at the other basin:

"You work that faucet and I'll work this one. We'll keep everyone out of the restroom."

Keith was afraid of getting himself into trouble and declined to help me, so I shot water at him, along with accusations of "Coward!" as he ran for the door. Then alone, with strong streams I held off every boy who tried to enter the restroom until the bell rang and recess was over. Waiting as long as I dared, at the very last moment, I slipped back into the classroom half-filled with the boys who couldn't pee before coming back from recess. I was quite amused when two or three of them later had to ask the teacher's permission to go to the restroom. I was pleased with the fun I had that afternoon, but trouble would arrive the next morning.

A half hour or so into our first class of the day, the principal of the school, Mr. Tucker, entered the front of the classroom carrying a baseball catcher's mitt. He spoke briefly to the teacher, then called my name.

"Carroll Moore. Please come to the front of the room."

"Yes, sir," I said, not knowing what he had in mind. I obeyed, went to the front, and he spanked me in front of the class using the catcher's mitt to protect his hand. The mitt fell off during the process, so he finished me off with his bare hand. His admonition to me, and indirectly to the whole class, was:

"Let that be a lesson to you, young sir. You are not to squirt water in the restroom."

I walked back down the aisle to my Karo desk with a red face, and surely a red behind, through a stunned classroom of kids. When I was seated, the teacher continued our history class as though nothing had happened, ignoring my "historic" spanking event.

At recess, I was surrounded by boys, most of whom had comments to make, and the others just wanted to listen. One smart-aleck boy from the Rosebud Community said:

"So, you're not to squirt water in the boys' restroom. Isn't that what we go there for?"

Another said:

"Karo, buddy, you're lucky he used the baseball mitt and not the bat."

And another:

"Got your Karo britches dusted, didn't ya?"

Most of the boys, however, were interested in the technique used to shoot the water so far from the faucet. I told them that Keith had helped to get it started, hoping to give him some credit. I then noticed that Keith was nowhere to be seen.

"Where's Keith?" I asked. No response.

Riding the Blue Bird home that day, I was pleased that I had crafted such a good water fight but hoping that my parents wouldn't hear of my troublesome behavior and subsequent spanking. I suddenly remembered that Sis worked at the school office for Principal Tucker. She was in the front of the bus with her friend Lilly May Bittle, and I was in the very back. *I'll talk to her on the walk home,* I thought. *Hope she'll agree not to tell on me.* When the bus stopped at Swaffer's store where we were to get off, Sis reminded me that she was going to the Bittles to have supper with her friend Lily May. *She may have already told them about the water fight since it happened yesterday,* I thought. My walk home was a troubled one.

The subject of the water fight wasn't raised at the supper table, nor afterwards. When Sis was delivered back to our house by Lily May and her dad, she went directly to the back of the house. I waited a few minutes before going where I was sure to find her—at Mother's dresser, in front of the mirror. She was a very pretty girl to begin with, and at the age when she had become interested in boys, was determined to become prettier, or even beautiful if that was possible. As I walked into the room, she was painting a surprise on her face using what looked like a thin pencil. Knowing I was the one who had to initiate the conversation, I started by saying,

"Your face looks pretty." I then asked, "Have you heard about my water fight at school?"

She smiled and said,

"Yes. Mr. Tucker came back to his office yesterday with the ball catcher's mitt and told me he had just spanked my brother—then told me why."

"You didn't tell Mother or Dad about it, did you?" I asked.

"No," she said.

"You won't, will you?"

"Depends," she said. "Someday I might ask you to keep a secret for me. Will you do that when I ask?"

It seemed like something in the far and distant future if it should ever happen. Of course I said:

"Yes. I will."

Having just finished both eyebrows, she turned her surprise from the mirror, and looking me straight in the eye, said: "You have to remember this. I'll ask you one day."

Again, I agreed. As I thanked her and left the room, I felt much lighter. That was the day I first began to appreciate my sister.

Riding to school the following day, I was making plans as the Blue Bird carried its load of plodders and seekers down the graveled road to Quitman. Keith must have told on me, I thought, although it could have been someone else, like any boy who couldn't get into the rest room that day. Or, someone may have heard the gossip and passed it on to a teacher, but I strongly suspected Keith and decided to confront him that very day. I found Keith toward the end of morning recess.

"You told on me about the water fight, didn't you?"

"No," he said. "I didn't."

"If you didn't, then who did?"

"I dunno," he said.

"Yes you do, and it was you. I'll get you for this!"

Recess was over before we could finish our business together, and I couldn't find the rascal during the noon hour. At the afternoon recess, I caught up with him, telling him:

"You told on me! I'll thump you good!" I started the fight with the first blow, and we fought with our fists, wrestled wallowing on the ground, then fought standing until someone in the surrounding knot of boys said: "Quick! Break it up! The teacher's coming."

We stopped fighting and mixed in with the other boys, and when the teacher got there, she couldn't tell who had been fighting, and, of course, nobody in the group knew anything about it. When the teacher left, I noticed Keith was slightly bent over and had a hand on his groin. One of the onlookers accused me of kicking him in the cods. This was a serious accusation. Kicking your opponent in the cods during a fight was the dirtiest trick of all and strictly prohibited by our code of conduct. If I had done so, the whole group might have piled onto me in retribution. I objected, saying I had done no such thing, and some of the boys agreed with me, and others didn't. As the arguments were getting hotter, Keith spoke up.

"He kneed me in the cods when we were wrestling, but he didn't mean to. It was an accident."

At noontime, some of us had been shooting marbles, and using my lucky taw, I'd won more marbles than my bag would hold and had them loose in both pockets. During the wrestling, I'd spilled them all over the ground but didn't dare to pick them up. I hustled back to class with the others leaving my winnings as scattered casualties on the battlefield.

Walking back to the classroom, I had the uneasy feeling that my foe had gotten the better of me, and I could feel a lump growing on my right cheek just under my eye. I was hoping it wouldn't be noticeable to the teacher, and it apparently wasn't. Later, taking the Blue Bird home, I was hoping my parents wouldn't notice it either.

Upset at the likelihood that my lumpy face might be discovered, I came last to the supper table and sat next to Grandma, who was at our house that night.

"You look bilious, Son. What's the matter?" she asked.

"Nothing's wrong, Grandma. I'm just fine."

She understood immediately that I didn't want to talk about it and let the subject rest. No one else at the table noticed my battle lump, and I knew already I wouldn't be challenging Keith to a re-match.

* * * * *

The day the midterm ended at Quitman School, I arrived home carrying my art prize in a paper poke, along with my report card just received that day. I had won the prize in our art class with a sculpture of a Trojan horse I'd carved from a bar of Ivory soap. Mother, going about her chores in the kitchen, gave me a snack while looking at my offerings. She marveled at the carved horse and the prize certificate with my name on it, which the teacher had made up with her typewriter, a half-sheet of paper, and a stick-on gold medallion. Mother seemed quite proud of me until she looked at my report card. Her expression was first quizzical, then serious. My grades were As and one B, except for math, which was a big fat D. It really was fat, written larger than all the other grades.

"What's happened with you in your math class?" she asked.

I didn't know how to respond. I couldn't explain what I didn't understand myself, so just told her I didn't know. I left and went out to play, knowing something really was amiss but not knowing what it was or how to deal with it. Receiving a bad grade must be much worse than I had thought.

After supper that evening, Sis went off to her room as Mother and I reviewed my report card and the art prize with Dad, who shared Mother's consternation about my grade. They probably thought they had a bright little boy on their hands, but here he was with a D in math. Dad wasn't surprised by my art award, as I was often whittling and carving with my pocket knife, and he helped me with crafts from time to time. He too was very troubled by the math grade.

"Needs to pay more attention and apply himself better" read the teacher's note on the report card.

From the note, it would seem clear I had been slacking off, but the other grades didn't reflect that, adding to my parents' puzzlement.

During the school break, Mother gave me some math problems to solve, and Sis helped with some more. The results confirmed I was slow in math, and that I sometimes transposed numbers within calculations causing my answer to be incorrect. While reviewing my other schoolwork, Sis also noticed that my spelling was pretty bad, noting that I reversed letters within words, and words within sentences.

When the next school term started, Mother spoke to my math teacher about my failing grade, and the teacher repeated what she wrote on my report card, adding that she thought I was a bit lazy. My parents encouraged me to work hard and study hard, which I surely tried to do. Fortunately, a different teacher taught my math class that term, and I did somewhat better, but my teacher, my parents, and I myself all knew that I still had a problem with math. What none of us knew then was that I had dyslexia, a learning disability caused by a dysfunction in how the brain processes information. I'm sure my parents had never heard of the condition, nor had any of my teachers. None of us knew that I had it, nor that it was a lifelong incurable condition.

For our family, my problem with math must have initiated a re-calibration of how life would proceed into the future, given that the eldest son had a learning disability that might impede passing the leadership torch to the next generation to keep us above poverty's ragged edge. Instead of calculating crop yield per acre, quantities of seed and fertilizer needed for the crops, and negotiating a good price for their sale, I would likely be doing art or crafts, singing songs, and telling tales—or just lollygagging on the front porch of the country store, strumming a guitar.

Previously, in one of his many setbacks, I heard Dad say: "This family will not be humbled to the dust!" He meant what he said, and I believed him in his serious pronouncement. My condition was, of course, no serious detriment to the family, which was infused with our dad's determination and included two other very promising children, but the paradigm was now reset.

I later managed passing grades in algebra, geometry, and trigonometry in high school, although with low grades in the subjects. The university math requirements were more challenging. My graduation was delayed a semester due to my extreme difficulty with calculus. Dyslexia entered the gates to my life along with the Trojan horse and remains there still.

THE WATCH OF THE WEATHER

Tornados are common in Cleburne County and feared by anyone with a lick of sense. Like poisonous snakes, they were part of the environment we lived in. Dad was responsible for "the watch of the weather," along with all the many other considerations relating to family safety.

What our parents and visiting family disliked most about our previous home at the Bettis Place was that it had no storm cellar. I can feel, even now, the quiet, collective undercurrent of fear welling up each time a heavy storm engulfed us. The storms start with a wall of black clouds standing solid as a rock-face across the sky, sometimes in an anvil shape. Lightning cracks and flashes incessantly, paired up with deafening thunder, and the rain comes down in torrents.

During one especially stormy night at the Bettis Place, Dad, in his hat and slicker, stood weather watch somewhere outside the house in a driving rain. He came back into the house from time to time to relate what he saw, which was nothing but darkness and flashes of lightning. With each flash, he tried to read the pattern of the storm, searching the horizon for the feared funnel cloud that could destroy us. As the storm intensified, he burst into the house streaming wet, leaned against the door fighting the wind to get it closed, and pushed a clothes trunk up against it.

"It's nasty black out there; can't tell a thing about what's going on," he said. "Had to fight to keep my balance against sheets of rain blowing sideways in this wind."

The decision had to be made whether to take shelter in the downstairs storage room under the kitchen or ride it out in the house. The storage room had two sides of stacked stone walls without mortar, and the end was a board wall and door. If sheltering there, Dad's fear was that the kitchen floor, the stone walls, and maybe the whole house might collapse on us, leaving us dead or injured with no way out. That night we slept in our clothes in the house near the fireplace, but I doubt that Dad got any sleep. We ended up never sheltering in the potentially dangerous storage room during the several other storms passing through.

At the Gresham Place, we were more confident in our prospects for survival, given we had a storm cellar in our backyard, out near the smokehouse. It was built halfway into the ground, with the excavated earth mounded up against its stone walls and covering the heavy timber roof. The slanted, wooden, double doors opened at the end facing our house. The interior had a dirt floor, and the stone walls were lined with shelves for storing canned and preserved foods. Long benches were built along each side wall for sitting or lying down for sleep. It was our provisioned survival hole and refuge from the besieging storms we knew would come.

We took to the cellar only twice, I recall. I don't remember much about the first time, as I slept through most of it, but the second time is still in my mind. Dad woke us up in the middle of the night and told us to hurry to the cellar. We wrapped our quilts around ourselves and followed him. I was impressed with the unusual scene. Dad was in front with Mother behind him, linking hands through us three kids back to Grandma. With both Dad and Grandma holding kerosene lanterns against the wet dark, we snaked our lighted way through the driving rain, from the back porch to the storm cellar. I shared a bench with my brother, sister, and a crock of sauerkraut. Dad had brought his ax, which he placed by the door in case he had to chop our way out through piles of wreckage. Although Dad seemed silent and serious, the feeling was relaxed and intimate with one lantern left lit. We kids fell asleep listening to stories told by Mother and Grandma as the storm raged around us.

Dawn broke the next morning to reveal our house and barn still standing, with no apparent damage anywhere, other than numerous tree limbs that had crashed to the ground. We left our refuge and returned to the house—our luck having held through yet another storm. On that joyful morning, I remembered how serious and quiet Dad had been during the night before with the storm beating at our cellar door.

Some years later, I came to better understood Dad's serious concern about tornados. In the safe remove of another time and place, he told me of his experience as a young man with the aftermath of a terrible tornado that struck Heber Springs, the Shire Town of our county. In 1926, it ripped through Main Street in late afternoon on the eve of Thanksgiving, destroying most of the buildings in town. That storm left the worst devastation Dad had ever seen, killing 19 people and injuring 75 others, some very seriously. At that time, he lived in the nearby Crossroads Township and went in with a rescue team. Working through the night, the first team of doctors, nurses, and their helpers focused on the injured and dying, dealing as best they could in the dark night with smashed bodies, severed limbs, and removal of the dead. The next day, Dad's follow-up team helped the remaining storm victims, removing them from unsafe structures, finding shelter for those who had lost their homes, and helping to find missing family members. Their efforts continued for days, clearing rubble-blocked streets and demolishing unsafe buildings.

He was fascinated by the storm's strange effects, describing in detail how livestock were lifted from one fenced area and dropped unharmed into another, and some people lifted and moved to neighboring properties uninjured. Other peculiar, unexplainable things included a straw driven into a tree without breaking the straw, and his favorite—a sharp, long splinter of wood driven through a stone jug and lodged there without breaking the jug. He could hardly believe he'd seen such things. He was awestruck, however, by the serious injuries and loss of life, and how much likelier people are to survive a tornado if properly sheltered in a cellar.

* * * * *

On Gresham Road, we were happy the storm had passed through without damage or destruction to our farm but heard from a neighbor that it had hit harder in other areas. That morning, I walked out to the road with Dad and Mother to meet Fatty Rankin, our RFD mailman, to see what news of the storm he might have. He arrived in his green Plymouth, spattered top to bottom with mud, and slid to a soft stop in front of our mailbox. He greeted us, handing out a bundle of mail.

"Has there been any damage from last night's storm in our area?" Dad asked.

"Yessir. A tornado went through near here and done some consid'rable damage. It smashed the Bettis rental place to kindling and took out a couple of barns, and maybe did more damage further south. Good thing nobody was in that house."

Mother and Dad looked at each other in what I thought was a strange way. There were no smiles of self-congratulation for our luck. Mother appeared to be almost wilting on the spot, but Dad put his arm around her waist, propping her up. As Fatty spun his wheels pulling away, they each took one of my hands, and we walked in silence back to our house. I'm sure they were thinking of how our world would have come to a tragic end had we not moved from the Bettis place when we did. As we reached the porch steps, Mother brought our thoughts back to the blessings at hand.

"We're having black-eyed peas with ham for dinner today."

THE FUNNIES

Dad loved newspapers. He read the Bible from time to time, but his real joy was the papers, which had been arriving at our household as long as I can remember. Mother liked them too, but magazines were more to her and Sis's liking. Dad told me about the different newspapers he had read, starting with *The Jacksonian*, then the *Headlight* as a second paper, then the two merged into *Jacksonian-Headlight*. I asked why a newspaper was named *Headlight*, and he explained that the Missouri and North Arkansas Railroad (M&NA) had come to town about then, which was a very big event. It was named after a rail engine headlight, not a car light. Dad read a Quitman newspaper when we lived at the Bettis Place but preferred the Heber Springs papers. The last one we read before leaving Arkansas was *The Cleburne County Times*.

The Sunday comics, or "funnies," as we called them, were a wonderful addition to the usual routine Dad had for my brother, Alder Lee, and me. He always awoke early, and on cold mornings, would light a fire in the fireplace, lay our boy's shoes on their sides with the opening facing the fire, and our socks on top ready for getting dressed by the fire. When we were slugabeds, he would come to our room: "Wake up you scalawags! Rise and shine!"

On Sunday newspaper days, after his farm chores, he'd walk down to the main road and pick up the paper dropped there by a deliveryman. We were always dressed and ready on newspaper days when he arrived with a smile and the fat newspaper roll, bringing in an aura of cold air and odors of the fresh outdoors. With the funnies spread out on the floor by the fire and a boy on each side, he read, and often explained, each comic strip as we all laughed. Some of our favorites were *The Katzenjammer Kids*, *Little LuLu*, and *Popeye*.

Some ten years later, one of Helen Marie's high school friends, Clotene Wright Bittle, visited her in California. Clotene then told me the most memorable thing about her many visits to our household on Gresham Road was awakening in the morning to hear the laughter of two boys and their dad, poring over the funnies.

Dad's love of the funnies has followed me and Alder Lee well into our lives. He awarded us nicknames after two characters in earlier comics he was fond of, but which we've never seen nor read. From little-bitty on, I was "Nip" and my brother was "Skeet," and we still are.

JEROME & ROHWER RELOCATION CENTERS

Early in July of 1942, Dad received notification from the construction company he had worked for on the Stuttgart Air Field that new government construction work was to begin in Chicot County. The company asked him to report as soon as possible to the construction company's field team in the town of McGehee in the southeastern Mississippi delta area. They requested that he bring any skilled construction workers he knew who desired immediate employment.

Dad was happy for the opportunity to have more outside income for the family and to do something to help in the war effort. He worked long hours for several days to get the farm in shape for a temporary absence, the length of which he didn't yet know. Once again, he left home with a suitcase in one hand and his orange toolbox in the other. But this time he was heading for McGehee, which was 150 or so miles from our home, half again further than his previous work at the Stuttgart job near Little Rock. He told us he might not be able to come home very often.

He hitched a ride to the nearby town of Pangburn to link up with Edward Evans, a carpenter he had worked with before, and bring him along to the new job. Edward knew another man in town, also named Edward, who wanted to come along and get a construction job. To avoid confusion, they called Evans Ed and his companion Eddie. The three drove to McGehee in Eddie's car. Upon arriving, Dad learned that housing for him and Ed would be there, and their team might work on not one, but two projects—the Rohwer Japanese Relocation Center in Desha County, and the Jerome Japanese Relocation Center in Chicot County. The two were thirty miles apart and their team would be moving between the two sites as needed. The superintendent assigned Eddie to another team.

When it seemed he'd been gone a very long time, Dad took a trip home for a short stay and to check on the farm. He told us that things had gone well on the job, and how encouraged he was by his team's capability. They had started construction of housing and related support structures for the two large facilities on remote, open, and somewhat swampy fields. His hardworking crews were all farmers with varying degrees of construction skills, but attentive and serious enough to learn. Besides Ed from Pangburn, other team members were from Lonoke and Faulkner counties, and a few from Pine Bluff. They started construction of footings for the buildings, even before the road team had graded the streets for drainage. As work started, those lacking in skills were paired-up with skilled partners, and all learned the old phrase, "time is of the essence."

Workers were expected to perform in several trades. The same team would level the building site; dig trenching for the foundations; build the wood forms; install reinforcing steel; mix, pour, and finish the concrete; then build the rest of the building. Combined trade skills were important, and training of the new workers had gone well. Their team was moving fast with construction, but the project was so large Dad couldn't tell how long it might take. The amount of work ahead seemed enormous. He didn't spend much time on the farm before returning to his job site.

After two or three months had passed, Dad came home again. By that time, he had been made team foreman and learned the full scope of their undertaking. After his promotion, he saw plans for one complex and learned the other was similar. Each of the camps, Rohwer and Jerome, sat on more than 10,000 acres, with the completed facility on half the acreage. Camp-operated farmland, timber forests, and open space was on the rest. The facilities were not going to be just housing, but two completely new small towns for a population of over 8,000 people each. Plans called for the housing to be arranged in blocks that would accommodate fourteen residential barracks, with each barrack having four to six apartments for the families. Each block was to have a mess hall, a recreation building, a laundry, and communal bathrooms. There were also buildings for schools, canteens, movie theaters, and gymnasiums. The administrative complex in each community included a military police station, a motor pool, hospital, warehouse, factory, and residential quarters for the War Relocation Authority (WRA) staff and military personnel.

Dad had, of course, also learned the complete purpose of the facilities, which was not just prison housing for Japanese prisoners as thought, but complete towns for the relocation of entire families of Japanese-Americans from the West Coast. He understood these internees were foreign nationals, but some might be American citizens. He was not as enthusiastic about the new construction job as he had been on his first return home. Mother thought he'd been working too hard and eating bad food, but she learned his reticence ran deeper. He and his team were concerned that the internees might be Americans of Japanese descent and were uneasy about the task they had undertaken.

Internees were being delivered to the camps by railroad while the construction was still under way. Many of the early arrivals were farmers from California, assigned to prepare the fields surrounding the fenced compound for row crops to provide fresh food for the camps. Others were assigned duties inside the compound. Dad and his crew encountered internees from time to time, many of whom they realized were farmers just as they were and spoke good English. Dad had long conversations with one internee about how to raise certain food crops in the local soil and in a climate so different from California. The work crews like Dad's had compassion for the Japanese, who had been ripped from the soil they tilled in California and brought there against their will. Later, however, as the barracks and service buildings were being completed and occupied, some issues emerged within the work crews, and in the small delta towns surrounding the two facilities.

As his construction crew was completing work on a mess hall, a food delivery arrived by truck and was being unloaded by internees. The construction workers were amazed at what they saw coming in the door. They had never seen so much good food at one time in one place in their entire lives. Dad, his team, and their families were subject to rationing of food and other items, and what they saw delivered was plentiful, but unavailable to them. The internees' shipped-in food was supplemented with the vegetable and fruit crops being grown in fields around the compounds. While the local population and the construction crews were restricted by rationing and whatever food family members still at home were able to grow for themselves, the internees were well fed with a diet of good food in the mess halls and canteens. They also had access to other rationed items, such as soap and name-brand cigarettes.

I'm sure Dad came from a more productive farm than many in his work crew, but he could understand the irony. No member of his crew had piped running water or a sewer system in their own homes. Their farms were accessible only by dirt roads, and Dad's was the only one of them with electrical service. But they were building a camp facility with electricity, showers, flush toilets, and graveled roads, movie theaters, and recreation buildings. It was troubling to them. They were torn between their compassion for the internees and what they saw as some form of favoritism. They found it difficult to reconcile how their government could treat the enemy internees so well and give no help to the poor dirt-farmers of Arkansas who had sons and relatives in the military, with many serving in the Pacific, and with family members dead, missing, or being held prisoner. They had sent their sons to the battlefields and were still struggling to recover from the Great Depression. At least some of them must have harbored animosity toward the Japanese internees for these reasons. But among the work crews, there seemed to be no overt antagonism toward the internees, according to what Dad could tell, although there were some incidents of hostility toward them within the surrounding delta towns.

There were occasional conflicts when the local townsmen had contact with camp internees, considering the "Japs" to be enemies and not welcome in or near their towns; there were reports of a local farmer having shot one of three internees who were outside the compound on a work detail with a camp supervisor. The farmer claimed to have thought they were trying to escape, and that their supervisor was helping them to do so. Other less serious conflicts were also happening in the surrounding towns.

Dad's co-worker Ed had run into Eddie of Pangburn, and the two caught up on what their respective work crews were doing. Eddie's team went into the small towns near their projects fairly often and the biggest news Eddie shared was an incident in a bar where he got into a fight. An argument started when local patrons were saying terrible things about the internee "Japs," who should be attacked on sight. Eddie was sure they hadn't even met an internee and argued they were shopkeepers and farmers like themselves and not dangerous enemies. He ended up with some bruises and a decision never to go into the local towns again. For Dad, Eddie's bigger news was that he had been trained on the job to become an electrician. That, Dad said, would help him from that day forward.

In 1943, with construction of Rohwer near completion, work crews were being reduced but work on the Jerome project was to continue through January of the next year. Although Dad was scheduled to continue, he chose to leave in mid-December to be home with family for Christmas.

"I'm done with Jerome," he said. "There are enough crews left to complete the job without me." It was an enormous relief for us all that he was, hopefully, coming home for good.

* * * * *

In discussing the projects later with family and close relations, Dad speculated on what might happen to the two towns into which so much money and effort had gone. At a family gathering, he said:

"I wonder what will happen to these new towns when the war is over, and it will be some day, hopefully soon. Will people like our work crews and the towns' local farmers be able to use those facilities our government has created or is this big effort useless?"

He may not have fully realized then that with the two projects, he and other workers had, from fallow land, created two of the largest agricultural communities in the state. He was, however, very detailed in listing the advantages of the communities as built. His recitation went something like this:

The Missouri Pacific Railroad and Highway 16 served both the towns and were available for transporting any farm products or timber to market. By Dad's estimate, almost 1,000 acres of land were under cultivation when he left the project. Most of the additional open space had been drained and made suitable for additional farmland. A large portion of the remaining open space was forested and available to produce lumber and firewood. A sawmill had been built and was operated to produce the lumber needed for construction of the buildings, which used only a small portion of the standing timber. The sawmill was still operational and ready for timber harvests and milling when operations were closed. The developed camps had all the facilities needed for thriving towns, including schools, movie theaters, meeting halls, industrial workshops, and housing for what had been a population of over 8,000 people in each of them. In addition to electricity, infrastructure included water wells, storage tanks, and a piped distribution system, which included fire plugs in the streets. They'd built sewage systems with piping and treatment facilities, as well as well-equipped workshop facilities with fabrication equipment, and a cannery operated for the food that was being grown. The motor pools had fuel storage tanks and garage workshops.

Dad thought the towns should be repopulated with farmers and support business owners. He described the ideas he had for using the housing blocks for a smaller population, combining the smaller apartments for more comfortable, larger dwellings. It was much later that I realized his concept was what we might call a farming cooperative where, as in some older European towns, the farmers live in the village, but farm their own parcels or communal land outside the village.

* * * * *

Dad had not kept in contact with his fellow workers and had no contact with the people in the towns surrounding the two camps. Several years after the war was over, however, he ran across Eddie of Pangburn who had kept track of the disposition of the government towns and had more information on how they had been initially formed. The government-owned parcels of land acquired for the projects, more than 10,000 acres each, had been tax delinquent lands needing clearing, leveling, and drainage to be of use for agriculture. Roosevelt's War Relocation Authority (WRA) acquired the sites with the assistance of the Arkansas Farm Security Administration (FSA), the agency in charge of the well-being of the Arkansas farming industry.

Eddie told Dad the sad story of the demise of the two projects they had helped to build. Rohwer, which had started operations September 18, 1942, was closed November 30, 1944. The Jerome facility, which started operations October 6, 1942, and was closed June 30, 1944, had operated a total of only 634 days. After their closures, the government used the Rohwer facility temporarily as a POW camp for German prisoners, after which both facilities with their buildings and cropland fell into ruin. The most troublesome thing to Dad was that the Arkansas Farm Security Administration, charged with promoting successful farming in the state, did nothing to protect the valuable resources of the projects for future productive use nor for the support of farming.

Except for the temporary employment for the development and construction of the projects, all the investments and efforts were lost. There had certainly been no benefits to the Japanese Americans who had lost their freedom and fortunes with their internment; the towns and counties where the projects were located did not benefit; nor did the citizens of the state and the U.S. taxpayers who had funded the debacle. Dad pointed out that from the creation by Roosevelt by executive order of the WRA to the wasteful abandonment of what had been created, all parties were losers.

Dad's final comments were: "What a waste. What a plentiful waste!" Following which, he never spoke of it again.

THE COUSIN'S WAR

It was 1942, and we were at war. Or, "at war again," as Dad would say. He hated war and said the luckiest part of his life, aside from marrying my mother, of course, was having been born too young for World War I and too old for World War II.

I was too young to understand much of what the war was about and why it was happening, but strong in my mind were the spectacles we saw in newsreels at the movie houses. These included air raids, bombings, aerial dogfights, and foot soldiers plodding through deep jungles. Mother and Dad sometimes discussed the progress of the war as reported in newspaper articles and on the radio, but didn't talk much about it, at least not with us kids.

I was fascinated by the wonderful war equipment—tanks, jeeps, submarines, and especially aircraft, without ever thinking of them as death machines. I had never seen anything so beautiful, dramatic, and exciting as the aircraft that the US, the British, and the Germans put into the European skies. Even the "Jap Zero" fighters in the Pacific were interesting. I somehow obtained model airplane kits and built as many replicas of these beautiful birds as I could. My cousin and I played war with our Radio Flyer red wagons, pretending they were jeeps and driving them through muddy ditches and "jungle" brush.

Mother's youngest brother, Urben Gresham, was excited with the notion of flying and went off to join the Army Air Corps and become a fighter pilot. I knew he had wanted to be a pilot, but when he arrived for a visit after induction, he was wearing a regular army infantry uniform. Mother later told me the whole story of the failed pursuit of his fly-boy ambition. He had described to her his arrival at the induction center, and how he could already see and feel himself in the cockpit of a Boeing Stearman Trainer, with its blue fuselage and yellow wings with the star-in-circle insignias on them. He considered himself a prime candidate for flight school. He was in good physical shape, with good eyesight, and not color blind, but the physical examination revealed he had an irregular heartbeat. He was both surprised and disappointed when they turned him away but was spurred on by determination.

Following a session with a doctor well known to our family, he applied at another induction center, full of confidence and a dose of digitalis administered by the doctor. Much to his dismay, the scheme didn't work, and he was again turned away. The digitalis, presumably, was to level out his heartbeat but may have had the opposite effect. Mother and Dad were amused that he even tried such a shot-in-the-dark caper and always wondered if the doctor knew all along what the result would be. Despite all this, they admired his fervor and determination. He served well in the military and, luckily, returned home safely, as did all our other family members who served.

THE FIRST HARVEST

After moving into the Gresham Place, our family faced many adjustments. Dad's work at the Army Airfield in Stuttgart had ended, allowing him to devote his full attention to the Gresham farm, which had lain mostly fallow for some years. We had arrived on the property in late summer, too late for most crops, but with repairs and preparation needed for the coming winter. With the help of Martin Trawick, our local horse trader, Dad moved our livestock to their new home in the barn. He then repaired the fenced lane for them, connecting the barnyard through cropland to the pasture in the lower meadow and stream. He made repairs to the house and barn, built a corncrib, and a garage for the Green Dodge. He rescued the orchard, disking down the weeds and opening the soil for the rain. He pruned every fruit tree on the property, even including the ornamental chinaberry and lilac shrubs alongside our house.

There was, however, little time between the end of Dad's job in Stuttgart and the intensive work on his next job at the Jerome and Rohwer Relocation Centers, which began that coming July of 1942. We harvested some fruit from the orchard—mainly apples—but the harvest was meager. After a year and a half at Jerome, with Dad home again, the months following his Christmas return were needed to prepare for a productive growing season approaching and what our family thought of as the first real harvest at the Gresham Place in the summer and fall of '44.

Dad completed his collection of livestock and poultry with milk cows, a calf for beef, pigs, and our usual draft animals. We had White Leghorn chickens, the very best for egg production, and Rhode Island Reds for the dinner table. He also considered getting some Dominecker hens, as he loved brindled, dappled things, and their grey-and-white feathers were a favorite of his. But he decided against them as they seemed too ornamental when he already had the Reds. I later realized that he may not have wanted to kill and eat his favorite ornamentals.

Useful items started appearing in our home, including an electric centrifugal cream separator, mail-ordered from the Montgomery Ward catalogue, and installed on the screened back porch. It was a great help in processing dairy products, giving a quicker start on cream for sale, and for butter- and cheese-making. One day, Dad surprised Mother with a used Maytag washing machine. He had heard tell it was available and bought it through verbal messages and hand-delivered cash, working through a delivery driver he knew with Zack Plant's Trucking Co. The washer had a square tub with rounded corners, and a wringer mechanism on top. It was a pleasant color green with a red-and-blue Maytag badge on the front. Mother loved it. A few months later, he brought home a new Norge refrigerator, with a freezer compartment complete with ice cube trays. Mother was overjoyed, as were we all. Now we could preserve food from spoilage, make ice for tea, and have an easy way to make ice cream in the summertime.

Mother increased her cheese production, making two-pound bars wrapped in cellophane, using a wooden Velveeta box as a mold. She sold the cheese at Carthyl Swaffer's store down on the road to Heber Springs. Her cheddar-like cheese, orange with a tinge of pink, became very popular. Not only was it delicious, but its homemade origin allowed sale without food ration coupons, further increasing demand. Mr. Swaffer sold all Mother could produce, which was 150 pounds that season.

Besides the useful equipment for food production, playthings also appeared. My brother and I each received a renovated, repainted bicycle, opening a whole new world for us. I had held the notion that having a bicycle was aspirational only, but here it was in my hands. Dad taught us how to maintain them with lubrication and repair punctures on the tires using hot patch. I was astride mine nonstop for a week after it was first rolled in. Another joy for the family, friends, and relatives was a new croquet set of lacquered hardwood with colored stripes on the balls and mallets denoting team markings. We all studied the rule book, learned the rules, and competition became keener with each set of games.

During the time we lived in the Gresham Place, the most important thing we purchased was a piano, which we got after our first year in the house. Mother had learned one of the women in the Olmstead family had one for sale and asked Dad to buy it for us. Mrs. Olmsted had bought it new, had it shipped from Boston to Heber Springs, and had maintained it well. We all loved music, and Sis had a particular gift for it. She had been taking piano lessons at Quitman School and could now practice at home, play her music, and accompany our singing. The piano was an upright of beautiful mahogany with ivory keys and an adjustable, ornate stool with bronze claw feet, each foot grasping a clear glass ball. We were quite proud of it, and it soon became the center of our family gatherings.

* * * * *

With row crops laid by for the winter and only the livestock and poultry to attend to, Dad started, for the first time in my memory, indulging in the joyful craft hobbies that began in his childhood. He was a whittler from an early age, as was his entire family. He began making windmills, whirligigs, and other playful devices. One such item was a little dancing man carved of wood with joints hinged by pieces of baling wire, suspended from strings like a marionette. Held by its strings, it danced on a paddle held between his crossed legs. We played with these items as they were made, and after producing multiple copies of them in different colors, we took them to Swaffer's store for sale.

One of Dad's fascinations was the Ole Bull Violin his grandfather had given him (once owned and played by the Norwegian virtuoso). During that winter, he set out to build a violin himself. Using a fine-grained wood of some kind, he completed a perfect-looking violin top, complete with f-holes and rolled edging, and a carved neck with the standard scroll fiddlehead. Time and opportunity didn't allow its completion, but we still have those first parts—and the old violin.

The farm was shaping up over the winter as we were mainly readying ourselves for the coming spring, a whole new season and our first *real* harvest at the Gresham Place.

* * * * *

With the bud-break of spring, white blossoms appeared like snow covering the thickets of green dogwood crowded along the stream branches. Our tulip poplar tree filled its limbs with large, pink-tinted, white blossoms, and everything came alive on the farm. We busied ourselves dealing with the cash crops of cotton, corn, and potatoes; with the livestock, the kitchen garden; and for the first time since the Jackson Place, with an orchard. To prepare for the coming harvest, boxes of Mason jars and even more boxes of tin cans and lids were stored in the smokehouse. Dad had purchased tin-canning equipment that sealed the lids, giving us two methods for putting up the fruits, vegetables, pickles, and meats.

For our first harvest at the Gresham Place, we had a bigger kitchen garden than I'd seen before, located in a fenced area between the smokehouse and the storm cellar. Once Dad broke ground and prepared the soil, Grandma Elizabeth came to visit and was a great help with the garden operations. The garden included a large variety of vegetables in sufficient quantities for our seasonal use as well as for canning and preserving for the winter. She planned her planting using different maturity dates for harvesting progressively with the heaviest harvest in mid-summer. Some root crops were to be planted in fall for winter harvest. She was our "plant whisperer," at one with growing things, and the vegetables always seemed determined to please her.

Before fruit and most garden vegetables appeared, Grandma brought me along to help in her search for poke salat, a wild green harvested and eaten like spinach. The early spring shoots are light green and need picking before they become older and too poisonous to eat. The leaves must be cooked and drained three times, as eating them raw or not well-cooked makes people very sick, although other creatures eat them. Birds love the dark red berries the plants produce later in the season, which are also poisonous to people. As Grandma wasn't yet familiar with the Gresham Place, it took some looking to scout out the grow-patches, usually along fencerows. We twice collected a "mess of poke," as she called it, for two meals, served with ham. Tasting like something between asparagus and spinach, the poke meals were one of our annual celebrations of spring. For our next spring and seasons to come, she memorized the location of the grow-patches we'd found and asked me to also remember their exact locations.

Following Dad's severe and long-needed fall pruning and tilling, the orchard burst forth with abundant fruit. For him, it was like a homecoming, having helped Grandfather Gresham plant the orchard some years before. Before planting, he even rescued the old Johnny Apple and mulberry trees that were originally on the site. The orchard peaches came in two varieties, one pink with aromatic white flesh, the most delicious I've ever tasted. The other, a yellow clingstone variety with firmer flesh, was perfect for canning as spiced pickled peaches. The two varieties of pear were as dissimilar as the Bosc and Anjou pears I'm familiar with today. We had several apple varieties, both a Red Delicious and a White Delicious, a variety with smaller fruit that was yellow with red stripes, and one tree of large green apples. As the fruit appeared, we ate the fresh ones and looked forward to canned apples, dried apples, apple sauce, and even cider. A row of berries along one edge completed the orchard. Adding to this bounty were the two big cherry trees near the chicken house and storm cellar, one red Bing and one yellow.

When the orchard was bright with fruit and the garden producing, our kitchen and dining room became a food processing facility. We had uncles, aunts, and cousins coming to help. Most brought food for the big midday dinner, and an uncle brought a stack of tissue-like pages from Sears Roebuck catalogs, calling them "apple wraps." The freshly picked apples were wrapped with the tissues and placed in barrels and boxes to be stored for winter.

Everyone helped with the canning and preserving, taking fruit, vegetables, and some of the preserves home with them for their own households. It was a tumultuous harvest, with so many people doing so many things. I later realized how well Mother and Dad had organized the event. They assigned whole families to specific tasks, so each team was already internally organized and ready to go. We had relatives from both sides of the family, and Grandma Elizabeth was overseer of the Moore crew.

I delighted in climbing the cherry trees with a cousin, gathering and eating the fruit while sitting in the tree limbs. With the "keek, keek" of the chickens always in the background, we first climbed the yellow cherry tree, then the red, always trying to pick more fruit for the bucket than we ate.

I thought it might be clever to ride a mule to the orchard and pick and eat fruit from my high mount. Dad gave me permission to take our mule Anthony to the orchard, so I bridled him and was joyfully on my way. Our first stop was the yellow apple tree where, from my mount, I reached for the nearest fruit. With my first bite, Anthony pulled the reins from my hand as he found the fallen apples on the ground too tempting to resist. I couldn't rein him up, so I dismounted and tried to pull him away with the reins, but he kept grazing on the fallen fruit. I had to walk to the house and get Dad to help me retrieve the beast from the orchard before he ate too much and got the colic.

* * * * *

Following the big harvest, it was Mother who suggested we also get help with cider-making by having a cider harvest event with friends and family. "With help," she said, "we can make more cider and have some fun doing it."

Dad agreed. "Yes. Let's do that. I've studied on it and thought of a way to make a cider press, so it'll be faster to make cider and give us more time to celebrate. You do the invitations, and I'll get started on the equipment."

I had watched and participated in the orchard harvest and was ready for this next event, which seemed to me like an echo of the larger one. Our cider was to be made from the orchard tree of large, green apples. Dad created the cider-making implements, including a wooden mortar-and-pestle needed for pulping, and a press, using the car jack from the green Dodge, for juicing. When the day came, we had an uncle and aunt, two family friends, and a neighboring couple on hand and ready to work. Dad and Mother assigned tasks for picking and for processing the juice. My job, alternating with my uncle, was pounding the chopped apples with the pestle to make the pulp. With the process finally done, everyone tasted the juice they'd produced, followed by a round of applause. We shared the juice with those who helped, so they could take home and drink raw or fermented hard cider. It was like a miniature harvest festival, which I've never experienced again.

* * * * *

The family gatherings that year were some of the most memorable in my childhood, with large dinners on the front porch, looking out across the lawn where the croquet court was set, games played, and scores carefully kept. But much of life during our years there has been lost from memory. We especially forget the more difficult aspects of life, like the hard work, heat, sweat, stubbed toes, blisters, cuts and bruises, snake encounters, chiggers and mosquitoes. But years later an occasional jolt of memory brings the more pleasant ones rushing back. For me, one such event occurred while reading a quote from Henry James, noted down and published by Edith Wharton:

> Summer afternoon, summer afternoon; to me those have always been the two most beautiful words in the English language.

James was, of course, referring to the ambience of English teatime in the summer garden. For me, the words brought back the image and feeling of iced tea on the front porch and games of croquet on the lawn of the Gresham Place with extended family and friends. Reading those lines, I even felt the humid cool of an afternoon when the summer sun has burned its way across the sky, sitting with siblings and cousins, crunching on large red crescents of melon, and spitting black seeds at each other.

Once, while sharing a Christmas meal with French friends in San Francisco, my own family meals came to mind. With the Pacific tide rolling in and a clear view of the Golden Gate Bridge in the distance, it was a different time and place for both me and my hosts, yet it felt like a familiar family gathering. I was being served duck confit brought from their family farm in the Dordogne, cooked and packed in its own fat to preserve it for the occasion. I thought of our family's winter meals of spiced pork sausage patties, fried and canned in their own fat in sealed fruit jars, preserved in the same way as the confit, and shared with friends and family in the same way.

The most vivid recollection of all emerged at an art exhibit I came upon by accident. During some years of frequent business trips to Washington D.C., I always visited as many art galleries as I could find time for. On one occasion, fighting the rain and cold, I made a random visit to the National Gallery, leaving my dripping raincoat and umbrella at the entry. An exhibit of watercolors by John Singer Sargent drew me in. One image depicted children in a green summer scene at dusk, playing among fireflies, romping in their white summer pinafores and short pants. To me they were enacting a summer family scene at the Gresham Place when we were visited by fireflies, or lightning bugs as we called them. After supper and the last lawn games, they came in great swarms, arriving with the fading of light. The darker it became, the more spectacular they seemed. We ran through swarms of blinking lights, captured them in pint jars to make glowing lanterns, crushed their tails, and painted their entrails on our cheeks like war paint. The adults sat on the porch watching the kinetic festival of lights produced by the bugs and five or six kids having the time of their lives. In the dead of winter, I'd found a Gresham Place summer of abundance at the National Gallery.

COUNTING CROWS

Dad and I were hunters in the snow that bright morning. The first snow of the season was a gentle fall over several days, leaving a foot or so on the ground. Warmer weather the day before had melted its surface just enough for the overnight freeze to leave a rigid crust on top. The sun was bright in the clear sky and its reflection off the crystalline snow produced such a blinding light we couldn't walk toward it. Beginning our trek with the sun at our back, we reasoned that our prey would be blinded, which would serve as our stealth tactic. Unmentioned, but what we both knew, was that every step we took broke the crust and made a noisy crunching sound warning any prey within earshot, yet we hunted on. The reason we gave for hunting was to bag a rabbit or squirrel—really more than one of either to make a "mess" worth cleaning and cooking. The real reason, I soon understood, was to have Dad teach me to aim and fire his .22 caliber rifle, and to spend some time with me before he was to leave again for work—this time in Michigan.

Dad's gun was a bolt-operated, .22-caliber, single-shot Remington he had ordered from the Montgomery Ward catalog, which had been delivered to our house some years before by the RFD postman. It had a heavy walnut stock, which helped to grasp and hold it steady for firing. He used it mostly for hunting small game and eliminating pests and snakes. He was a very good shot and was prized as the shooter when he and neighbors joined together for killing and butchering hogs almost every fall after the first frost. Dad hated to see animals suffer and knew how to drop the hog with one sure shot, rather than having him run around squealing, frightened, requiring several shots for the kill. Dad advised his neighbors that a bad slaughter also ruined the meat.

A flock of crows flew past and scrambled across the ice-covered branches of a nearby tree—a scattering of deep black shapes on the stark, white landscape.

"Let's shoot a crow," I said.

"Naw, let's not do that," he said. "We don't eat them, and they're not bothering anyone here in winter."

"Have you shot them before, like in the summer?"

"Yes, I have, especially in the spring of the year when I'm planting crops, and sometimes when I'm harvesting peanuts. They watched me planting rows of cotton seed, then followed behind me digging them up and eating them. I took my rifle to the fields and started picking off the little thieves. They began waiting until I left my field to come back and forage. I then started coming back often, which kept them at bay for a while."

"They must be pretty smart," I said.

"Yes. They're very smart. When plowing up peanut vines for harvest, a single-crow lookout alerted the flock that followed behind me eating the nuts. People have found crows can count up to five. The peanut thieves learned that if only two or three were eating the peanuts, I wouldn't bother to stop plowing and shoot them, so they kept their numbers down. The crow flock and I got to know and understand each other, and I could identify some of the individual crows. After I'd planted cotton seed, they would post a sentinel to alert the others when I'd left and was some distance out of sight from the field. I once looked back and saw the single pilot crow in a tree over my field, but out of distance for a good shot. I aimed my rifle at him, raising it slightly for distance and fired. To my surprise, the shot took him down. It turned out he was the lookout crow I'd come to recognize by a gap in his wing feathers.

"Once, after shooting a crow in my cotton patch, the flock came back and held a crow funeral; something I'd never seen before. The usually noisy flock came in complete silence, alighting in a tree near their dead. They stayed still and silent for quite some time, then flew away without making a sound. They saw me there but knew I wouldn't shoot them while they mourned their dead. We've no reason to shoot the crows today, not even for target practice.

"See that pine at the edge of the woods? There's a pine cone on the lower right branch. Draw a bead on that cone."

On my second try, I hit it and other designated targets for the day. We crunched our way home having bagged no game but declared it a successful marksmanship hunt. As we entered the kitchen, Mother asked: "Any game today?"

"No," I answered. "Just target practice so I can get some next time."

With a knowing smile, she said: "We still have lots of ham from last night's supper. Get yourself warm, son."

KNICK-KNACK ENTERPRISES

Dad had heard tell there were jobs available in the Michigan car manufacturing plants and was preparing the farm for his absence on another outside job, the length of which he was yet to know. On the day before leaving for his job search, he gave me a bundle of craftsman's supplies to busy myself with while he was away. These would also be a birthday gift, as my birthday was coming soon. Most important of these items was a book entitled *The Young Craftsman*, which is still in my library. Its green, cloth, hardcover binding impressed me when I received it, and its contents even more so. Included were plans for small craft projects of all kinds for young people and also larger projects, like building wooden boats, which would require help from adults. In my nine-year-old boy's hands, it seemed much larger, but the color of green still seems the same.

Dad and I reviewed it together and selected two projects of ornate knick-knack shelves for displaying small memorabilia. One was to be hung flat on the wall and the other designed as corner shelves. The designs were imposed on a square grid system to facilitate transfer of the pattern to a larger full-size grid of one-half-inch squares. Dad helped me transfer the pattern to full size for the corner shelf, so I would know how to do it for the other projects I might select.

The tools in his package were a hand scroll (coping) saw, a small handsaw, and a small drill for making "entering" holes for the saw blade. Materials in his package were sheets of quarter-inch-thick pine wood, sandpaper, wire brads for nailing the parts together, a small can each of shellac and varnish, and two brushes and solvents for cleaning them.

A week or so following Dad's sad departure for Michigan, I began my crafts projects working after school and on weekends. After completing fabrication and applying varnish or shellac finishes to eight of them, I set out to sell them at fifty cents each—my first attempt at direct marketing. For portability, I bundled them with heavy twine, slung them over my back, and started my long walks to neighboring farms. They were well received, especially by the women in the households, and I sold several straight-away. In selling my first production, I learned the most demand was for the corner shelves with the darker varnish finish. With such long walks from one farm to another, and with my next walks to be even further from home, I arranged with Carthyl Swaffer at our local country store to allow me to sell the next batch of shelves on the front porch of his store to customers who came in for gas or groceries. Mr. Swaffer was impressed with what I was doing and allowed me to store the shelves in his back room. The Blue Bird school bus dropped us kids off next to his store every school day, and I tried to sell some shelves on his porch before going home, but Saturdays were the best sales days. As the cold winter deepened, I stopped my craft work, which was done mostly on our front porch. I had some inventory, so I continued my sales.

People started buying my shelves for Christmas gifts, and on one Saturday I spent most of the day on

Swaffer's porch completing my sales. He gave me a candy bar to go with the dinner sandwich I'd brought from home. For the last three sales, the buyers gave me a dollar instead of a half. The last sale was to a man from Heber Springs, who bought it for his wife as a Christmas gift, for displaying her Hummel figurines. I didn't know what Hummel figurines were but was happy to get the dollar. Following the last sale, I said:

"Thank you, Mr. Swaffer, for letting me sell my shelves on your porch."

He replied: "It was good doing business with you, young Junior."

Walking home, I realized the "business" was all one way. My crafts weren't a big money-maker but earned me some spending money, and I enjoyed creating the shelves and was pleased people wanted them. I'd saved back one knick-knack shelf as a Christmas gift for Mother, which I was hiding in the smokehouse. It was a corner shelf with an extra coat of dark varnish.

A CHILDHOOD CHRISTMAS ON GRESHAM ROAD

I arrived home from school one cold day to learn we had a letter from Dad saying he was coming home for Christmas. This would be a good Christmas after all. Mother read the letter to me, which said: "I'll be coming home for Christmas and won't be coming back to Michigan. When the sun goes down every day, I want to be with you and with our kids."

Dad's job in Michigan was doing assembly-line work in the Guide Lamp Division of General Motors. He vowed never to repeat that experience, which he found to be an exilic purgatory. He couldn't bear to be separated from family in remote work locations any longer, and the Michigan job was the last work he did away from home.

After reading his letter, Mother said: "We're going to make this the best Christmas, we've ever had."

And so she did. The holiday events had never started so early, and there were never so many of them in one season as this Christmas on Gresham Road.

At Quitman School, we drew names in our homeroom class so that each student would receive one gift from another, and no one was to disclose whose name they had drawn. On the last school day before the holiday break, a Christmas program was held in the gymnasium where a large tree was decorated with tinsel icicles, red roping, and colored lights. Our music teacher presented a brief recital with her singers, then the house lights dimmed, and tree lights made brighter while everyone sang Christmas carols, accompanied by our music teacher on the piano.

Back in our homeroom, the teacher distributed our gifts, followed by more carol singing. I don't recall whose name I had drawn, nor what gift I gave him or her, but will always remember the gift I received, and how it surprised me. It was from Keith, the boy I had fought with earlier in the year. I thought it very odd he'd drawn my name ticket from the grab basket. I opened the beautifully wrapped, small box to find a pearl-handled pen knife, which I was very pleased to have. It was rolled inside a note which, in excellent penmanship, read:

"Merry Christmas to my Sparring Partner Karo."
From Keith

How could this be? I bullied him in the boys' restroom at the beginning of our water fight, and afterwards, accused him of tattling on me and picked a fight with him. Here he was behaving like a friend as though none of this unpleasantness had ever happened. I wasn't big on social graces, to be sure, but knew I had to thank him. I caught him in the hall just outside the classroom door as we were all leaving for the day. It was a simple but, for me, important exchange of words:

"Thank you for the knife, Keith. It's a very nice one, and I really like it."

He smiled and said: "You're welcome, Karo. Have a Merry Christmas."

With the new knife re-boxed and in my pocket, I was still thinking of Keith, and of Christmas, as I boarded the Blue Bird for my trip home. I slid into the seat next to my classmate Elmer Simkins. He was very smart in class, yet always looked like something the dogs had dragged in. His blond hair, like scattered straw, was always "stabbled," a term used in our community for "tousled," and his clothing disheveled and sometimes even dirty—something we seldom saw.

I suspected he wasn't getting much help from his mother, and especially not with the dinners he brought each day. Most of the students had sandwiches made with sliced light bread, while some had biscuits or even cornbread. His biscuits were homemade, but not made in the usual way with a biscuit cutter and baked in an oven. They looked like random-sized, large piles of dough dropped into a skillet of hot grease, the final products ending in the shape of small, odd-sized cow-pies. Today, Elmer hugged a long loaf of Wonder Bread, holding it up from time to time to inhale the odor of the "good stuff." He was given money to buy the bread during noon hour and bring it home as a special treat for his family's Christmas dinner. I shared his joy in finally getting some of the "good stuff" his family might have had only once a year. I wished him Merry Christmas as he left his seat and stepped down from the Blue Bird at his bus stop. With a spring in his step, he started his walk home holding the loaf against one side of his face.

* * * * *

The Christmas tree was the next event in our holiday procession of rituals. Dad and I hiked to the field behind our orchard where he had selected a tree at the edge of the woods. It was a red cedar he picked out earlier in the year and pruned occasionally to perfect its symmetry. Dad had been working out of state and was anxious to see it again. When we found it, he said:

"Look at that. It's a perfect cone shape with dense foliage and the right size for our living room. It'll smell good too."

After sawing through its trunk just above the ground, we each took a limb and dragged it bottom first through the snow, all the way to our front porch. He fashioned a base of one-by-four-inch boards on edge in a pinwheel pattern and attached them to the trunk for strength and stability. His height assessment was correct, and the tree stood in our room with the tip four inches from the ceiling. And Dad was right—the wonderful smell of cedar filled the room. Mother had already stacked the boxes of decorations on the floor near where the tree would stand. We had tinsel icicles, colored glass balls stored in boxes like eggs in a crate, red roping, multi-color lights shaped like candle flames, and a lighted star for the top. After dinner, Christmas would start in earnest with the decorating of the tree.

* * * * *

Our household was already excited about this year's Christmas celebration, as it would be a big one. At Christmas, we usually had short visits with a few members of both sides of our family over a period of several days, most often at their houses. This year, almost all members of Mother's family came to our house. I couldn't remember this ever happening before —never all together and never all at our house. There would be Granddad Gresham; Uncle Joe, Aunt Merle, and their kids, Joanne and Roland; and Uncle Guy, Aunt Kathleen and their son, Billy Gene. In addition to all these nearby relatives, this year Mother's brother Wendell and wife, Annie, and their three kids were driving up from Louisiana; her sister Evelyn and husband, Hershel, were coming out from Little Rock; and even the newly wedded Uncle Erben and his bride, Madge, might possibly attend. Most important to my sister, brother, and me were the seven or eight cousins coming along with them, all about our own ages. There were days of excitement and preparation.

* * * * *

Our next event was a Christmas pageant sponsored by Uncle Guy's church, in which he was to participate. It was being held at the McAnear Church, located near our uncle's homestead. His big part in the pageant was the role of the innkeeper, who had no room for Mary, Joseph, and baby Jesus. Although his spoken lines would be all of two sentences, we were quite pleased to have an actor in the family and would certainly be there to support him. We were hopeful of seeing him backstage after his performance to tell him how very good he was. Dressed in our Sunday-best, we piled into the green Dodge; braved muddy, rutted roads; and in low gear, ground our way to the church, jumping over mud puddles as we disembarked.

Inside, the walls were decorated with cedar boughs, pine cones, and red ribbons. At one side of the low stage, a cedar Christmas tree was all decked out with blue lights and covered with "angel hair," the spider-web-like decorative netting. As the house lights dimmed, the tree took on a soft glow with deep blue light spreading around the entire surface of the tree. I thought the effect was magical, especially when the program began with the singing of "Silent Night, Holy Night" with the house lights off.

The pageant went well with not a single actor forgetting their lines. Uncle Guy, the innkeeper, was dressed in Holy Land garb, which looked very much like his bathrobe. The first of his famous lines was to tell Mary and Joseph:

"There is no room at this inn."

Following their visit with the shepherds, the three wise men arrived. Leaving their camels back-stage, they appeared at the village inn searching for Jesus and asked:

"Where is this newborn child, Jesus, who is to be our king?"

Uncle Guy, the innkeeper responded with his second line:

"I know not."

At the end of a flawless presentation, the curtain call drew enthusiastic applause. Each actor walked to center stage, spoke one of his or her short lines, and left the stage accompanied by applause. The most important actors appeared first, followed by the lesser roles, the innkeeper being last. With an important presence, Uncle Guy walked to center stage, faced the audience, and spoke his line:

"I know not."

The audience went wild with applause as he made his bow. Each time he tried to leave the stage, the volume of applause swelled again for more bows. The church pastor finally had to intervene and close the show. Uncle Guy was surrounded by fans, congratulating him on his acting skills. When we finally got close enough to greet him, Dad asked for his autograph.

* * * * *

On the morning of Christmas Eve, the pace of food preparation and holiday decoration at our house quickened noticeably. One bedroom, stocked with scissors, tape, ribbons, and wrapping paper, was reserved for anyone who wanted to secretly wrap gifts. The kitchen was now ablaze with cooking and baking. All local families were to help with the food preparation, and each was to bring some part of the holiday meal to be assembled at our house on Christmas day. As hostess, Mother busied herself preparing the Prince of Wales cake.

In all our family Christmas dinners, the meats, poultry, and vegetables have varied, but Mother always displayed the Prince of Wales cake as the central feature. No one remembered how the tradition got started, as all in our extended family have known it since childhood. It was a yellow, three-layered cake with spices, nuts, and dried fruits folded into the dough. It had a white icing between the layers and covering the outside of the whole cake. The outside icing, heavily sprinkled with grated fresh coconut, reminded me of a deep, fluffy, winter snow.

In the afternoon of Christmas Eve, most of our preparations were completed. Our tree was fully decorated, and the Prince of Wales cake sat proudly on the kitchen table, surrounded by bowls of cookies and fruits. Our local Gresham relatives—Uncle Guy, Aunt Kathleen, Uncle Joe, Aunt Merle and their two families of kids—had helped with the day's activities and stayed on with us to greet our Louisiana relatives, whom none of us had seen for several years.

During our wait, a radio weather broadcast gave warning of an ice storm building over most of Cleburne County, where we lived, and part of the adjacent Faulkner County—both in the travel path of our expected visitors. This report caused us to worry for our already overdue travelers. After a trip to the barn for his chores, Dad told us the puddles of snowmelt in our yard were freezing over with the temperature drop. Our local Gresham guests decided to leave before dark and hopefully get home before the roads iced over. Darkness fell, with still no sign of our Louisiana relatives. We were concerned that Uncle Windell, Aunt Annie, and their three kids might be stranded somewhere in a ditch or freezing at the side of an impassable road.

We were preparing for supper when there came a pounding on the front door. It startled us because it was so loud, but also because it was at the wrong front door—we had two of them. Dad opened the door to find Uncle Wendell standing on our front porch, holding a flashlight.

"We almost made it all the way, till we got to your steep hill, which is all ice," he said.

The two of them took kerosene lanterns and loaded rope, trace chains, and toe sacks into the green Dodge and drove to the hill. They shackled the chains together, added the rope, and connected the front bumper of the Dodge on top of the hill to the front bumper of Uncle Wendell's Ford below. Dad threw toe sacks under the drive wheels of the Ford to give them traction. With the Dodge in reverse and the Ford in low gear, they gradually eased the car up the icy slope and onto the level part of the road.

When the cars reached our yard, Dad came inside and said:

"They're here. Get your coats on; you've got to see this!"

The visiting family had to leave their car through the driver's door, as the passenger door was frozen shut. Out they came—Uncle Wendell, Aunt Annie, and cousins Thomas Harold, John A., and Peggy Jo. We were greeting them on the front porch when we saw what Dad meant by "you've got to see this."

The car, a black '34 Ford two-door sedan, was now a white, ghostly apparition glittering in the lantern light. The family had been driving through heavy rain and snowmelt as the temperature plummeted, and the whole car quickly iced over. The wind swept the freezing water backwards causing a white glazing of ice over the whole car with trails of long icicles projecting off the back. Though the car was standing still, the frozen image of its speed made it look like it was in motion. The wire-spoked wheels bristled with ice crystals extending out six inches or so in geometric patterns, like huge, three-dimensional snowflakes. We all walked around and around the car with lanterns and flashlights, amazed at what we saw. Uncle Wendell stood beside his spectacularly decorated car as an artist would stand by his sculpture at a gallery opening. He presented the car with a gesture.

"This is our decorated Christmas gift to you all. Merry Christmas!" he said.

After supper and some visiting time in front of the living room fireplace, sleeping spaces were arranged for the visitors. My brother and I gave up our bedroom to our uncle and aunt, and joined our sister and three cousins in the front bedroom. A fire was left burning in the fireplace to break the chill. The two girls took the bed, and the boys bundled up and slept on quilt pallets spread on the floor. With thoughts of "Christmas is tomorrow" in our heads, we slept soundly.

On Christmas morning, we were awakened at first light by my brother, Alder Lee, who leapt from his pallet and streaked across the room in his Long Johns shouting: "Christmas! Christmas! Christmas!" The room erupted, then emptied as everyone, in their underwear and some dragging their quilts, ran through the connecting Shakespeare room to the Christmas tree in the living room. I thought we were the first up, but Dad was already there with both the fireplace and tree lighted. He calmed us down and told us the story of a childhood Christmas when he received a pair of Buster Brown shoes as a gift, and how proud he was to receive them. He loved that they squeaked as he walked. This story bought some time for the adults to appear one by one, carrying their cups of coffee and each saying "Christmas Wish" as they entered the room. This was another Christmas season tradition of our family—saying "Christmas Wish" instead of "Good Morning" when entering a room to join other people at the beginning of the day. It always began two or three days before Christmas, and as with the Prince of Wales cake, no one knew how the tradition started.

"Are you ready for the paper-tearing?" Dad asked.

We, of course, were, and excitement built again as he donned a red stocking-cap, declaring himself Santa Claus, and designated Peggy Jo with a green cap as his "delivery Elf." Between the ho-ho-ho's, he read the name on each gift, handing it to the elf for delivery. The first gift I received was a toy metal car with rubber wheels—the biggest toy car I had ever seen, much less owned. It was a red station wagon about twelve inches long with a simulated wood body. It was a fantastic gift, and I could hardly wait to take it outside and push it around. I anxiously waited for my other gifts, which were two model airplane kits. Each kit had section parts and long rib material stamped on thin sheets of balsa wood, and green tissue paper for the outer skin. In a separate bundle was a very sharp Ex-acto knife with extra blades to cut out the parts, and tubes of airplane cement to glue them together. I was proud to be able to identify the types of airplanes from the pictures on the boxes—they were a Curtiss P-40 fighter plane and a Mitchell B-25 light bomber. I knew already that model airplanes would be much more fun than the Victorian knick-knack shelves I'd just built the months before.

As the "paper tearing" wound down and wrapping material was being boxed for reuse or thrown into the roaring fireplace, I bundled up and ran outside to play with my new toy car. I pushed it a few feet along the grass, trying to resist the temptation to run it through two mud puddles, frozen over with thin ice, in the swale beside our driveway. I ran it through both and was immediately sorry. Returning to the house with my muddy toy, I hid it in the corner behind the Christmas tree to avoid any required explanation of why I'd dirtied it. I didn't know why myself, but it sure was fun. During the excitement of the day, Mother pulled me aside and told me how pleased she was to receive the knick-knack corner shelf. "I'll keep it forever," she said.

* * * * *

Later Christmas morning as guests started arriving, I couldn't believe the bounty being heaped on our household for the big celebration. The food offering was astonishing. Along with the home-grown pork, beef, and poultry as well as our local bounty from garden and orchard were a variety of nuts and cookies. Our seldom-seen favorite exotic and tropical items, including oranges, walnuts, almonds, Brazil nuts, and coconuts, were with us again. Desserts were being added to a side table next to a punch bowl of eggnog.

With so many children under foot, we were all assigned tasks to busy us while the meal was being readied. Some of the older kids were sent to haul firewood and pine-knot kindling to be ricked up on the front porch. With two fireplaces going for the crowd of revelers and an active kitchen stove, a big supply was needed. Cousin Peggy Jo and I were assigned nut shelling duty. She and I were of even age, born only days apart, and always got on well together. There on the floor, beside the warm fireplace, we were each given a hammer, a block of wood, and a shared bowl of nuts. Some of the shelled nuts were to be used for cooking and some for snack bowls, and we were told not to eat any until done with the job. The hickory nuts were too hard to crack, and even harder to get the meats out, so we focused on walnuts, almonds, and pecans. None of Peggy's nuts seemed to reach the finish bowl. She ate them as she cracked them. When she started eating the nuts I'd cracked, an argument ensued. I grabbed the bowl and said,

"Stop eating those nuts."

The argument ended only when I hit her on the head with my hammer. This bit of drama ended our task. I was reassigned to help some older boys haul in wood and lay the fire in the front bedroom fireplace, while Peggy Jo was sent to help in the kitchen.

At gathering time, everyone tried to crowd into the living room, but many spilled over into the dining room, and a few peered through the kitchen door. Dad and Mother welcomed the guests before the eggnog was passed around and the music started. With Helen Marie at the piano, and Alder Lee and me standing beside her, we led the singing with every Christmas carol we knew.

The holiday table was like none I'd seen before. The centerpiece was a sugar-cured ham from Dad's smokehouse, beside a fruit-stuffed roasted chicken, and a roasted goose with boiled goose eggs circling it on the same platter. There was some of every vegetable grown in our gardens over the past summer and fall. We took plates and filed past the shimmering plenty of the Christmas table where Mother and two aunts helped serve. On another table, waiting for later, were the desserts, including apple and pecan pies and, of course, the Prince of Wales cake.

Guests took their food and scattered throughout the house sitting on all our chairs, the beds, and some even on cream cans brought into the kitchen. We children were sent with our plates into the front bedroom where we gathered around the fireplace. A new fire had just been lit, and we sat on the floor eating, talking, and watching as the hot pine-knot kindling spit and crackled, setting light to the fat logs above. I remember that feeling, sitting by the fire with my brother, sister, and cousins, eating our Christmas meal, and knowing that all was right with the world. I even told Peggy Jo I was sorry I hit her on the head with the hammer.

After desserts were served, the music began again, this time with a different theme. We sang all the top-ten hit-parade songs for the past few years as the party continued. Missing the backup bands of Guy Lombardo, Stan Kenton, or Harry James, we still tried to sound like Jo Stafford, Bing Crosby, and Judy Garland with only a piano behind us.

It seemed no one wanted to leave. But finally, food was packaged to take home, and before anyone left, we gathered around the Christmas tree and sang "Silent Night" one last time.

For me, this was the most memorable Christmas I've ever had, and I believe those who attended the party always remembered it as well. What my brother, sister, and I didn't know at the time was that this would be our last Christmas at the Gresham Place. It was unclear at the time whether we would leave our home or not, but the other family uncles and aunts came together for Christmas just in case. In the late spring of the coming year, our family moved to the California Central Valley to start a new and very different life far from all the family who came to our last holiday gathering on Gresham Road.

1945

PART IV. THE GREAT MIGRATION

THE GREAT MIGRATION

It was in the fall of the year 1944 when Grandad Gresham came by to visit us and talked about California. He had just returned from several months there with his brother Rob. I later believed his frequent trips to California were for a travel adventure and change of scene, but his stated purpose was to work various jobs in the annual fruit and vegetable harvests. He arrived at our house in mid-afternoon and hungry. Mother offered him the remains of a meal of ham, peas, and turnip greens left over from our dinner. Grandad was pleased at how our family had shaped up the farm, with repairs to the barn, construction of a car garage, and repairs to the house and storm cellar. He was also pleased to see the orchard had been brought back to productivity, commenting that Dad had helped build the house and plant the orchard, and had just refurbished both.

When Dad joined us for supper that night, there was discussion with Grandad about how well his brother, Mother's Uncle Rob, was doing in the town of Atwater, in the Central Valley of California, and of the opportunities there.

* * * * *

At the Gresham Place in late May of the following year, we enjoyed a spell of nice spring weather. Upon returning from school one day in May, I removed my shoes and socks on the front porch and walked barefoot down the road to see what work the WPA had done earlier in the day. The rain had just stopped, and I walked in the muddy road, splashing in rain puddles, and noticing the fresh rilling on the newly built slopes. The WPA work crew had been rebuilding parts of the road during the week, and my self-assigned job after school each day was to visit the construction site, check on their progress, and bring home any food left in cardboard boxes by the crew. Both Mother and Dad knew Wayne Starr, boss of the work crew, who didn't like to see food wasted, and was generous with whatever food the crew didn't need for the day. They sometimes left a loaf or two of bread, which I brought home for us. I was near our house carrying back a damp loaf of Wonder Bread when I heard Dad calling me in. I was curious why, as it wasn't yet time to sit down for supper.

As I entered the dining room, Dad, Mother, and my brother, Alder Lee, were seated. Sis came into the room and joined us. After a short pause, Dad began.

"We've got something to tell you kids. We're planning to move. I've studied on it, and your mom and I have talked a lot about it. We've decided to move our family to California."

Dad explained to us that he and Mother had learned from the Greshams, the Moores, and from one of his cousins from the Coe family that it seemed like a perfect opportunity for us. Other talks we kids hadn't yet heard included those with Mother's cousins living near Uncle Rob when they'd come back for visits. Dad had also been in touch with his Uncle Robert E. Lee Moore, who was also considering a move to California.

They had all reported that jobs there were plentiful, paid well, and there was a big demand for construction workers. After questioning all of them, Dad was also convinced that the education system was better there than where we currently lived and would be a good place for us kids. Both parents were big on education, which was a contributing factor in their decision to move.

"I think we'll have a better life in California, and a brighter future there," Dad said. "Especially for you kids."

* * * * *

This would be a year of many changes. A month earlier, I had a new and unforgettable experience. In April, during our school day, students were told to gather on the paved area under our flagpole. With all students and teachers present, they held a memorial for our deceased president, Franklin Delano Roosevelt. The solemn ceremony included lowering the flag to half-mast and the reading of a text by our school principal, Mr. Tucker, which ended with a prayer. I had never experienced the death of a relative or anyone else I'd known. I understood that I had only one grandmother, on my father's side, and one grandfather, on my mother's. I knew the other two had died, but then, at my young age of nine, it was so many years before I was born, I thought that was just the way things were. The ceremony for our deceased president impressed me and caused me to think about death for the first time. I had yet to experience anyone's death, yet I somehow felt the grief of those surrounding me at the flagpole. With our move to California, leaving our home and extended family, I was soon to feel a different grief, one of separation in both a personal way and sharing that of our parents and other family members.

In early May, another event that connected us more to the world at large was the surrender of Germany, ending the war in Europe. In the discussions among our parents, friends, and other family members was a thankfulness that it was over, and that our surviving servicemen would be coming home. There were many questions as to what this would mean for our future. And we were still at war with Japan.

We had not discussed the decision to leave Arkansas with any members of our family other than Granddad, who provided most of the information about our destination so familiar to him. The biggest impact of Dad's announcement was on my Grandma Elizabeth, who had never traveled far from home. She was born in Carroll County and moved to Cleburne County with her father and brothers and hadn't traveled beyond any adjacent county since her arrival as a child. Our California destination was like the ends of the earth to her. In fact, it seemed to make her physically ill. On a visit to us shortly after Dad had told her of our plans, I found her sitting alone in the front porch swing, not swinging, just sitting still and looking distressed.

"What's the matter, Grandma?" I asked. "Are you sick?"

"No, son, I'm not sick. I'm just down in the mulligrubs. I'm sad because you're leaving."

Later that day, also on the front porch, she had another discussion with Dad about our pending move.

"This is like talking to the winter winds," she said. "Why can't you reason with me? If you quit farming, your family will starve to death."

During the conversation, she majestically spread her arms as if to encompass the entire farmstead and said:

"Where, under heaven's arch, will you find such a place as this?"

Dad pointed out that we didn't own the place and never would and wasn't sure he could keep it going without outside work opportunities, which had almost disappeared. Dad promised that when settled in California, we would send for her, and she could spend part of each year there with us.

Other members of our families were still on their farms with additional outside work arrangements, or out of farming altogether. Mother's brother Wendell had moved to Louisiana some years before and owned several sawmills. She was very close with her sister Evelyn, who lived in Little Rock with her husband, a manager with the U.S. Postal Service. Other uncles were into forestry management, timber harvesting, and another worked in an icehouse, was a deputy sheriff, and a breeder of hunting hounds. Most family members advised us against leaving, but Uncle Wendell, who had already moved away, thought it seemed like a good opportunity for us. Dad's last work outside the farm was at that dreary place in Michigan, and he hadn't found other work nearby.

I was surprised, but not distressed, to learn that we were moving. School would be out soon, and Helen Marie would graduate from high school. She was already wondering what the future had in store for her and seemed ready for an adventure. As children, we were happy to follow our parents' lead and were ready for the move. We had no notion of all we were leaving behind and of what we would be losing. For us that would all come later. We would soon miss the love, caring, and constant support of the extended family that surrounded and supported us. These things were so much a part of our lives it never occurred to us they would vanish.

After returning in later years to visit our former home, I realized how difficult it must have been for our parents to leave Cleburne County, with its sweet ambience of springs and streams among gently rolling green hills, and the forests where Dad could name the variety of every tree, shrub, and bird in the landscape. More importantly, loss of the community of family, friends, and the unspoken comfort of knowing, or knowing of, everyone in the local townships from birth, must have been devastating to both, especially for Mother. She was the default verbal historian for our family and could reel off the begats of most other families in our township and several of those surrounding ours.

* * * * *

Dad arranged for a farm auction and for our family to travel by train to the California town of Atwater, where we would stay with Mother's Uncle Rob until we found our own place to live. Uncle Rob was the California anchor for our family and seemed well established there. Once the family's mischievous black sheep, Rob was now a preacher. Not only had he found the Lord, but the ideal career for a born storyteller: tell a story once a week and people give you money. His sideline was buying, refurbishing, and selling old, dilapidated houses.

Although many of my childhood memories are indelible, I have no recollection at all of the auction of our household, farm equipment, livestock, and the many items given away, such as canned foods, sugar-cured hams of meat, and slabs of salted bacon. This may have been because my brother and I were likely placed elsewhere with relatives so as not to be underfoot at the auction, nor to suffer the trauma of seeing our hard-won possessions disappear. With all totted up, we were flush enough for travel and a grubstake in the Promised Land.

My memory returned with our arrival in Little Rock for an overnight stay with Mother's sister Evelyn and her husband, Herschel. The next morning, they dropped us off at the railway station with nothing but the clothing on our backs, a suitcase each, and a basket full of food. With a tearful separation, they hugged us, put us aboard the train, and waved us goodbye. Once on the train, Mother seemed troubled and uneasy, but Dad was keeping the conversation positive.

"We'll follow the sun," he said brightly. As the train gathered speed, he even seemed elated. "We're running like Ol' Andy," he announced, referring to our former, troublesome mule who claimed his freedom by breaking free from the auction yard and running far away.

We sat in rows of two and changed seats from time to time to keep us kids from fighting. A sixth seat was occupied by our food basket. We had brought hams, cheeses, and jars of canned fruits and pickles to Little Rock where Aunt Evelyn helped prepare the travel basket. In the early evening, Mother, who sat next to Sis, began quietly sobbing. Dad asked Sis to trade places with him, kissed Mother, took her hand, and tried to encourage her as best he could. We slept sitting up in our seats. The next morning, Mother seemed better but still uneasy with our situation. Sis was also unhappy. She had seemed ready for our move until the school term was over and her high school graduating class held a picnic and swim event on the river at Tumbling Shoals. Socializing at that event heightened the feelings of friendship and bonding that had developed between her and her classmates through their twelve or more years together. Realizing she was losing all this had saddened her almost to tears, but I could tell she was trying to appear brave and support the family.

The train travel was uneventful and somewhat depressing. Our passenger train was often side-tracked as troop trains and shipments of military equipment had priority. We were delayed for hours at a time, as we watched flat cars carrying jeeps, tanks, and large containers painted the army color of olive drab. It was dizzying to spend time standing still as trains moved fast alongside of ours. Often, it felt like our train was moving when we knew it was standing still. Occasionally, we would learn what state we were in, but it all looked the same, seeing mostly cargo on the other tracks.

The travel was boring for me until we reached California, when Dad told us we would see something special up ahead. He was very interested in what's called the "Tehachapi Loop," where the train climbs to the top of the mountain pass. We were excited too, and especially when we saw it. To gain elevation the train climbs in a spiral loop over its own track. At our stop at the bottom of the mountain, as the engineer was adding another engine to our train to get more power, the passengers filed into the railway cafeteria for breakfast. Our family went through the food line together but had to split up to find seating. I had my first meal in California seated at a table with strangers. I found the food tasteless but didn't mind. During my meal, I had my first encounter with the individual size, waxed-cardboard milk carton, which looks like a gable-roofed house—something I'd never seen before. I didn't know to unfold the little roof at the gable end. My tablemates watched as I searched for the hole to drink from but offered me no help. Finding no opening, I surprised them by retrieving my Barlow from my pocket, cutting a top corner off the carton and drinking my milk.

We reboarded our train, which began its climb to the Tehachapi summit. We were on the best side of the coach to see this phenomenon and looked down on the other end of our own train. As we watched in amazement, Dad shook his head and commented: "I can't even guess, how the engineers figured this one out."

Our descent down the western slope of Tehachapi delivered us to the flat, expansive farmlands of the Central Valley, which was impressive to us with its size and burgeoning croplands and orchards. As we clickety-clacked our way up the valley, we discussed the future at our new home. Dad said he would "hit the ground running," giving me a visual glimpse of him jumping off the still-moving train and running along beside it before it stopped. He clarified by saying he would buy a car, find a job, then find a house to rent. Helen Marie would try for a clerical job, and Mother and I would work in a fruit harvesting, packing, or canning job, one where we could take six-year-old Alder Lee along with us. The harvest season was just beginning, and we were confident we'd find jobs.

Our arrangement was for Uncle Rob to meet us at the train station; we were hoping he had gotten the day and time right. If not there, we would call him on the telephone. It was late afternoon when we stepped off the train with our luggage and entered the station to find Uncle Rob standing just inside the doorway. After hugs and handshakes, he explained that Aunt Anna hadn't come along to greet us, as we might not all fit in the car. He loaded us and our luggage into his Chevrolet, with Dad riding shotgun and Alder Lee perched in the place behind the gearshift. He drove us to his home, a tidy, three-bedroom house in the east part of the town of Atwater. Aunt Anna had a meal ready for us, and our stay with them started as a small family reunion in their dining room. We methodically followed the program Dad had outlined on the train.

Within days, he had bought a black, 1930 Chevrolet sedan, and within a week he had a job as carpenter for a construction company that was just starting a housing subdivision east of town. Sis quickly found an office job at the nearby Merced Army Airfield.

* * * * *

For the first several weeks with the Greshams, Mother and I hadn't yet found a job. This, I'm sure, was a bit trying for Aunt Anna, who wasn't used to having kids around, and therefore, trying for Mother as well. I had the country-boy habit of climbing every tree in sight and started with a Chinese Pistache in the Gresham's yard. My monkey trick of swinging from a limb brought both boy and limb crashing to the ground. I was accustomed to tough oaks and hickories, not realizing the crisp brittleness of the ornamental. Mother disposed of the limb and apologized to Aunt Anna for the damage.

Alder Lee and I were fascinated with the water faucets and garden hoses. We learned we could push a running hose into the sandy Atwater soil and, under water pressure, it would keep burrowing its way in as long as we kept pushing. Sometimes the hose would resurface somewhere and shoot water up like a fountain, accompanied by our applause. After a busy afternoon, we had worm-holed the lawns in front and along one side of the house, when we buried a hose so deeply, we couldn't pull it out. Trouble followed, as we had to wait for Dad to get back from work to help retrieve it. Hoseborings were then forbidden. We had to stop our "fog dancing" too. In some afternoons just at twilight, the mosquito abatement truck would drive slowly through the streets leaving a misty fog of insecticides in its wake. Along with some neighborhood kids, we would follow the truck, running and dancing back and forth in and out of the fog. During the second such event, they caught us and forbade this activity too.

I'm sure Dad was trying to break quickly from any further reliance on Mother's family, and the annoyance to them of having kids around, so our first rental was a temporary one—a small cottage on a peach farm, a mile out of town. The bad-boy antics of my brother and myself probably hastened the move. After moving, I realized I missed Uncle Rob, as he had become a favorite storyteller. After some weeks there, Mother and I started work back in town in a cutting shed for apricots. The fruit was cut in half, pitted, and the halves arranged on large wooden trays placed side by side in the drying yard for the sun to work its magic. We then moved back into town, renting our first California house.

EPILOGUE

– 188 –

Our first house in California was on Grove Avenue in the east edge of the town of Atwater. Dad rented the house from a retired Portuguese farmer. It was on the same large parcel as the farmer's own residence, and Dad and the owner agreed to share the large garden area, each with his own plantings. The house was small and cramped, but a good start in our new location, and we were happy to have our own house again. It had no particular style or character and was unremarkable in every way except that it was ours. It felt temporary to me, and I'm sure it felt so to the rest of our family.

We were trying to adjust to our surroundings, but much seemed missing from our lives. Although we had cousins of both Mother and Dad living in nearby towns, we missed the weekly family gatherings and interactions with friends and neighbors. There was no socializing with family on an almost weekly basis, no croquet games with cousins, no holiday family gatherings, no Fifth Sunday singings and no contact with school friends nor any mechanism to stay in touch. In fact, there would be no first cousins, uncles, and aunts; some we wouldn't see again for years. And only on occasion would we see our grandparents. It was especially difficult for Mother, who missed all the visiting we were so accustomed to as well as her close relationship with her younger sister, Evelyn. They often wrote to each other and made occasional phone calls, but it all seemed so distant.

Dad referred to our homesickness as a "pining for Pearson," our hometown. Mother wondered when she would ever see her sister and brothers again.

Conversations about a trip back to Arkansas didn't go far as we needed to work and to establish ourselves in our new community. It was the wrong time to buy expensive train tickets, and our 1930 Chevrolet wasn't reliable for such a long trip, so we resigned ourselves to staying put with hopes for a future trip.

One day, Dad found Mother silently weeping while writing a letter to her sister Evelyn. He noticed it when she moved her writing paper so her falling tears didn't splotch her blue-ink messages. She then wept openly and loudly in his arms. Following that, they decided to subscribe to the newspaper they were reading when they left our Gresham Place home: *The Cleburne County Times*. Mother arranged for a subscription to the paper, which was mailed to us. With the paper arriving—a rolled cylinder with a mailing label—each issue was read through and through by both Mother and Dad, and they continued their subscription for many years.

However, there were also some positive discoveries after our great migration. Mother and Dad, both from families that had done a fair job of coaxing food from the soil for many generations, were amazed at the robust food production surrounding us. We were now in an irrigated, sandy desert, and they could hardly believe the bounty it produced. On a Saturday afternoon while shopping in downtown Atwater, our whole family stood on a street corner adjacent to Highway 99 silently watching the 18-wheelers lumber past, stacked high with lug-boxes of fruit or bins of vegetables, all headed for processing plants. The rail line parallel to the highway had a rail spur lined with refrigerator cars waiting to be loaded with fresh fruit and vegetables. Mother broke the silence.

"This must be that 'fruited plain' we've heard so much about." Mother's humor was always welcome, but I sensed uneasiness among us all about our future in this new and different land. In many ways, there was promise that our lives would be better than before, and, buoyed by our parents' sense of humor, we bravely faced the future. But we did so with a lingering sadness for all that had been lost.

– 192 –

About the Author

William Carroll Moore was born in Cleburne County, Arkansas, and moved with his family to the Central Valley of California at the age of ten. He holds a bachelor's degree in architecture from the University of California at Berkeley and a master's degree in urban planning from Athens Technological Institute in Greece. After practicing architecture and planning, he taught both subjects as a professor at the California Polytechnic State University at San Luis Obispo, CA. He now lives in the Napa Valley of California where he writes fiction and nonfiction. His short stories appear in the anthologies: *Meritage, Collected Works from Napa Valley Writers 2019, Napa Valley Writers' Third Harvest 2021*, and *Opus IV NVW 2023*. He has contributed articles to a regional newspaper, to the *California Writers Chapter Newsletter* and has published in the *Quarterly Journal* of the Cleburne County Historical Society. Mr. Moore is a continuing guest reader for "The Storytellers," a literary program for the public radio station KXCT-FM in Vallejo California, as well as a contributor to "Lettuce Listen," a story program at station KDVS-FM in Davis, California.

APPENDIX:
PRINCE OF WALES CAKE RECIPE

Ingredients

CAKE

1 Cup	Butter
1 Cup	Sugar
4	Eggs
1 tsp	Vanilla
1 Cup	Molasses
1 Cup	Buttermilk
21/2 Cup	Flour
1 tsp	Baking Soda
1 tsp	Cinnamon
1/8 tsp	Salt
1 Cup	Raisins, ground.*

*Dates, dried apricots or prunes can be used instead.

1 Cup	Nuts, chopped
1 Cup	Coconut, shredded

FILLING

1 Cup	Milk
2 Cups	Dark Rum
1 Cup	Nuts, chopped
1 Cup	Coconut
1 tsp	Vanilla
2 Cups	Sugar
1 Cup	Raisins, ground

Method

CAKE

Preheat oven to 350. Beat butter and sugar. Add eggs and beat well to ribbon stage. Add molasses and beat until blended. In separate bowl combine dry ingredients. Sprinkle ¼ Cup over nuts and raisins Alternately add dry ingredients and milk with vanilla added in it. Add nuts and raisins. Batter will be very thick. Divide into three 9" layer cake pans and bake until pick inserted in center comes out clean. (about 40 to 50 minutes). Cool.

After cooling, place layers in container with tight-fitting top, sprinkle with rum evenly over each of the layers. Close container and place in cool area for 3 days.

FILLING

Cook milk and sugar to soft-boil stage. Cool to warm and beat well. Add nuts and ground raisins or dried fruit of your choice. Spread between layers and on cake to seal all crevices. After icing is completed, cover cake surface with shredded fresh coconut.

Cover and set cake in cool area for 2 days for flavors to develop and mix well.